BOTANICAL WREATHS

Nature's Glory in Appliqué

LAURA
MUNSON
REINSTATLER

CREDITS

Editor-in-Chief .... Barbara Weiland
Technical Editor .... Kerry I. Hoffman
Managing Editor .... Greg Sharp
Copy Editor .... Liz McGehee
Proofreaders .... Tina Cook
Kathleen Timko
Design Director .... Judy Petry
Text and Cover Design .... Joanne Lauterjung
Photography .... Brent Kane
Illustration and Graphics .... Laurel Strand
Stephanie Benson
Laura M. Reinstatler

Botanical Wreaths ©
© 1994 by Laura Munson Reinstatler
That Patchwork Place, Inc., PO Box 118, Bothell, WA 98041-0118
USA

Printed in Canada
99 98 97 96 95 94   6 5 4 3 2 1

Library of Congress Cataloging-in-Publication Data
Reinstatler, Laura Munson,
    Botanical wreaths / Laura Munson Reinstatler.
        p.   cm.
    ISBN 1-56477-056-7 :
    1. Quilting—Patterns. 2. Patchwork—Patterns.
3. Appliqué—Patterns. I. Title.
TT835.R45   1994
746.9'7—dc20   94-17052
                                                      CIP

MISSION STATEMENT

WE ARE DEDICATED TO PROVIDING QUALITY PRODUCTS THAT ENCOURAGE CREATIVITY AND PROMOTE SELF-ESTEEM IN OUR CUSTOMERS AND OUR EMPLOYEES.

WE STRIVE TO MAKE A DIFFERENCE IN THE LIVES WE TOUCH.

That Patchwork Place is an employee-owned, financially secure company.

DEDICATION

This book is dedicated to my mother, Ruth Chaffee Munson, who taught me how to sew and to appreciate things botanical; to my father, Carl Munson, who taught me an enjoyment for words and humor; to my son, Colin, who loves my quilts; and to my husband, Bob, who has provided the means all these years for me to indulge my love of quilting.

ACKNOWLEDGMENTS

This project has been a joy to work on from the first drawings to the final bleary-eyed tussles with the computer! There are many people whose help and support were invaluable to me and to whom I am deeply grateful:

To Vickie McKenney for her vision, inspiration, and courage; and to shop owners Delberta Murray, Julie Stewart, Diane Coombs, Sharon Yenter, Mary Hales, and Laura Wilson;

To Nancy Chong, Heki Hendrickson, Mary Lyons Camden, Sue Pilarski, Chris Walsh, Jane Palsha, and Mia Rozmyn, a special thank you for their hard work and for sharing their breathtaking quilts;

To Noreen Havens, who kindly shared her blackberry flower and red alder–cone techniques;

To Verna Zander for her botanical research;

To my Botanical Wreath students, who have inspired and taught me so much;

To Charisa Martin, Tina Garreis, Jean Cook, Carol Porter, Theresa Burkhart, Pat and John Robertson, and JoAnn Gove for their love and pats on the back;

To all the special people at That Patchwork Place, including Nancy Martin, Ursula Reikes, Susan Jones, Janet White, and of course, Marion Shelton for her fabulous hugs; and most especially to Jo Lauterjung, Laurel Strand, Brent Kane and Stephanie Benson for making this book beautiful, to Kerry Hoffman for her unfailing humor, support, and commitment to this project, and to Barbara Weiland, whose belief in me has given me more than she'll ever know;

To Marsha McCloskey, Liz Thoman, Sara Nephew, Mary Hickey, Joan Hanson, Marty Bowne, and the rest of the Monday Night Bowling League for their inspiration and encouragement.

And for their patience during the final hectic month of writing, drawing, and stitching, thanks especially to my husband, Bob, for making his own hamburgers and trying to explain DOS and other computer mysteries to me, and to my son, Colin, who's a great kid.

Most of all, hundreds of bouquets and thank-yous to Joan Dawson for her generous help, her unfailing support of my work, her spectacular quilts, and her unbounded enthusiasm for quiltmaking and, most especially, appliqué. She is truly a dear and wonderful friend.

Table of Contents

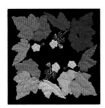

*Thimbleberry,
page 51*

*American (Red)
Mulberry, page 54*

*American Sycamore,
page 56*

*Carolina Laurelcherry,
page 58*

*Cascara Buckthorn,
page 60*

*Bluegum Eucalyptus,
page 72*

*Pussy Willow,
page 74*

*Flowering Dogwood,
page 76*

Ginkgo, page 78

*Horsechestnut,
page 80*

30" Medallion, page 96

Eastern Redbud, page 62

European Mountain Ash, page 64

Garry Oak, page 66

Salal, page 68

Vine Maple, page 70

Magnolia, page 82

Tulip Tree, page 84

English Holly, page 86

Red Alder, page 90

Blackberry, page 93

INTRODUCTION

Two years ago, students in one of my Twelve Days of Christmas, block-of-the-month classes were finishing their thirteen-month course. They lamented that the yearlong series of meetings was ending. Not only had they learned a great deal about appliqué but they had become fond of each other. I suggested that we begin a new block-of-the-month appliqué project to continue in the same time slot (third Monday of the month). Their enthusiasm inspired me to design a new series of blocks.

We decided that we wanted to do a botanical-type wreath series, so I designed wreaths using leaves, flowers, berries, and/or seeds of locally growing shrubs and trees. Eventually I included trees from other regions of the country. I created a new look by departing from the stylized motifs of other beloved traditional appliqué patterns.

With the support and encouragement of Vickie McKenney, owner of The Calico Basket in Edmonds, Washington, where I do most of my teaching, I began the third Monday class with the new series, which we named "Botanical Wreaths."

Each month we began a new block and soon we were "oohing and aahing" over another appliqué quilt in progress. My students marvel at how their appliqué skills have improved during the time that they have worked on their wreaths. Now, as this first class nears completion of their wreaths and borders, they are again asking me, "What's next?"

At first glance, the quilts in this book may appear complicated or even intimidating. Each 15" wreath includes leaves, seeds, berries, and/or flowers which, in total, appear to be overwhelming. However, the appliqué pieces in these wreaths have been designed so that, while they look realistic, the curves and points are not different from most stylized appliqué.

Some of the blocks are simpler to appliqué than others. The level of difficulty is indicated for each quilt, so that you can start with the easier ones and work into the more challenging blocks.

Take time to plan your quilt so that it best suits your needs and taste. It is a lovely showcase for appliqué and quilting and will display your skills wonderfully. If you use colors that make you sing, you will enjoy every stitch you take in your legacy quilt.

Laura Munson Reinstatler

DESIGNING YOUR QUILT

With the wreath designs included in this book, you have many options. You can make a quilt as intricate or as simple as you wish. All twenty wreaths surrounding the large central medallion, plus the intricate borders, make a very impressive work of art. Choose a portion of a wreath to embellish a garment. Wind one or more of these motifs over a shoulder of a dress or blouse or on a skirt hem for a dramatic look. Enhance a synthetic leather or suede belt beautifully by grouping leaves across the front. Or, add a quadrant to the flap on a purse or bag.

The Design Wall

Using a design wall during the planning stages of the creative process is very important. I cannot stress strongly enough the advantage of putting fabrics, colors, and completed blocks on the wall to study while you are designing. When you step back and use a reducing tool to view the entire work, you can better assess the balance and overall quality of the design.

I will never forget one student who, when nearly all her blocks were completed, put them on the wall in class for the others to see. She gasped when she saw the impact of her work. Despite my continued efforts to stress the importance of designing on the wall, she had never before put her blocks up on a wall. Although she was delighted with her blocks and their effect, she noticed one block stood out so much that she decided to redo the entire block. Had she auditioned her fabrics on the wall with the other blocks, she would have saved herself the extra work.

For each new block, I pin up all my completed blocks, plus a background block to which I begin pinning fabric scraps and colors in the areas to be appliquéd. Along with making sound design choices, I have a chance to admire my work, further motivating me.

Two things are important about a design wall: You must be able to stand away from it to get a view of your entire project, and you must be able to pin your blocks and fabrics to the surface. Insulation board, available at lumber stores, can be fastened to the wall and is perfect for this use. Paint the wall white or cover it with white felt or flannel. (For years, I worked on a white flannel blanket that was fastened to a wall with push pins.)

Deciding Which Blocks to Make

There are a number of ways to display the Botanical Wreath quilts. Make a quilt with a single wreath to hang on the wall or combine several wreaths to create a larger wall hanging or bed quilt. Hang a group of four differently colored blocks, representing each season, or change seasonal quilts every few months.

Include different wreaths in your quilt, or repeat one wreath several times for a more traditional look.

Set the blocks as squares or on point. By alternating on-point appliquéd blocks with plain fabric blocks, you can show off your appliqué and quilting skills together.

A 30" medallion-type wreath, combining many of the species found in the 15" wreaths, is designed to be used as a separate quilt or to be surrounded by other blocks. Adding the appliqué borders designed for this medallion makes it a showstopper!

Spend some time thinking about the overall effect that you want to achieve, the statement that you want to make, and how you want to display your quilt. Since the wreaths and medallion are designed as units that can be used singly or in combination, there are numerous ways to make your quilt a very personal statement.

Choosing the Border

Border designs vary the look of these quilts, too. Two basic appliquéd border designs are included; a wide (12") border and a narrower (6") border. Of course, you can design your quilt with wider borders by expanding the appliqué patterns a bit.

This quilt stands on its own with plain borders. Use several of the colors from the block or repeat a coordinating print in the border for a different, yet equally effective, look.

Border a single-wreath quilt with a single strip or multiple strips of coordinating fabrics. Or, piece a border

in the pattern of your choice. Create a stunning appliquéd border by using motifs from the block.

Selecting a Quilting Design

Quilting patterns for the quilt can be as simple or as intricate as you wish. A traditional gridded quilt pattern beautifully enhances the appliqué without competing with the intricate design. If you include large areas of background fabric in your design, adapt one of the wreath patterns to use as a quilting pattern.

Wreath Colors and Values

Because the quilts in this book require a significant amount of time to complete, make every moment a pleasure by choosing colors you love. I always encourage my students to select fabric colors that they consider a self-indulgence. Watching the colors overlap and blend adds to the joy of creating each block.

Restricting color choices to only a few hues gives the quilt a strong, graphic look. To get a rich, complex effect, use a variety of coordinating colors.

Try creating the illusion of light hitting each leaf in a slightly different manner by varying the values (the degree of lightness or darkness of a color), creating depth within each block. Enhance the dimensional effect by overlapping leaves of a lighter value against darker ones.

To identify the value of a fabric, place it with groups of light, medium, and dark fabrics. Stand back, squint, or look at the fabrics through a reducing tool. (See page 13.) My favorite method is to view fabrics through a red "value finder," such as the Ruby Beholder™. The red "filter" allows you to determine the fabric's value. This method is especially helpful when you are working with many gradations of value.

Varying the tones or intensities of colors creates dimensional effects as well. Warm (reds, oranges, and yellows) and/or clear colors appear closer, while cool (greens, blues, and purples) and/or grayed colors recede.

Create the illusion of light falling across or illuminating the quilt by manipulating the color and value so that each block appears to have its own light source. Grade each block within the quilt from light to dark, to achieve an overall spotlight effect in your design.

Single block

Quilt

Before you commit your needle and thread to fabric, it is helpful to lay tiny snips of your fabrics in wreath configurations on the background fabric to get an idea of the overall effect. Do this on your design wall and step back to get an overall view of the blocks. Use this technique to fine-tune your choices for each block.

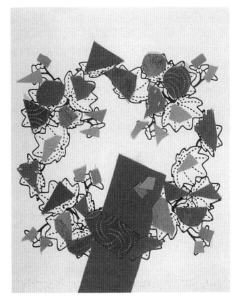

Explore and play with color to find many stunning effects. Take time to browse through this book and use the quilt photos for inspiration. Be creative and even daring for whimsical, unexpected, or otherwise satisfying results!

Selecting Fabrics

Selecting fabrics is one of the most fun aspects of designing a quilt. Pulling the colors and fabrics together, deciding value transitions, and watching the magic begin is heady stuff! I make major design decisions initially but keep an open mind to other color and fabric possibilities as the quilt progresses.

Background fabric plays an important part in the quilt's overall effect. Choose colors and fabrics that support the appliqué without distracting from it. Selecting a small-scale, textural design with a limited range of hues and values usually yields more satisfying results than using a large-scale, highly contrasting fabric. The wreath's leaves should show clearly against the background; while a dramatic contrast is not necessary, the leaves shouldn't be lost against the surrounding color or print.

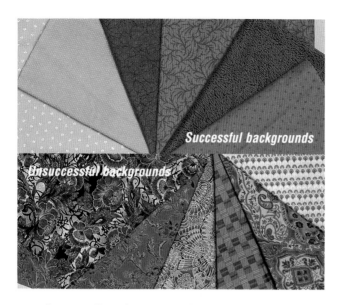

Successful backgrounds

Unsuccessful backgrounds

Some quiltmakers vary their background fabrics within the same quilt. A scrappy look using two or more small-scale prints in the same color range works well. Background squares of different colors, related to each other in hue but varied in intensity (from clear to grayed colors) or value (light to dark), add drama. Dividing each background square into two triangles and arranging the triangles into patterns through careful planning creates a striking quilt. See Heki Hendrickson's quilt on page 43.

Fabric print characteristics provide a vast array of textures. Use them to create fascinating and realistic effects for leaves, berries, flowers, and seeds.

Window templates help you spot special effects that you would have never considered by simply looking at the large piece of fabric. Use these windows to select fabric areas that look like leaf veins or to find shaded areas of berries. I find it helpful to make a generic leaf and berry win-dow on a 3" x 5" card and take it along when shop-ping for fabrics.

Make specific window templates for each piece in the wreaths you plan to make. After using this method, you will find yourself selecting fabrics in a completely different way than you did before. Directions for making window templates are on pages 14–15.

Be careful of how you combine textures. Like background fabrics, highly contrasting print structures can create a "busy" effect, obscuring the design and interrupting the continuity of the wreath. For the projects in this book, the best prints are those with lower contrasts and medium- to small-scale designs. However, you may find a perfect piece in a larger print scale when you use the window template.

I use 100% cotton fabrics because they are easier to turn under for appliqué. Cottons, silks, and wools all work well with the wreath patterns and can be slightly forgiving if small discrepancies occur during appliqué.

Felt or nonwoven synthetic suedes work well for small appliqué pieces, such as berries and seeds, because they require no seam allowances for small, intricate pieces. Just cut on the seam line and appliqué. For economy, purchase felts and synthetic suede scraps.

Preparing Fabrics

Prewash all fabrics that you use in this quilt. You will spend a significant amount of time in making your quilt; it would be tragic if it shrank or if colors bled into each other when the quilt was laundered.

To make sure a fabric is colorfast, rinse each fabric in a tub of clear, cool water until there is no color left when the fabric is removed from its "bath." I have found that the more water I use in the rinses, the faster the fabric rinses clear. Do not soak for long periods of time.

If the fabrics are not preshrunk beforehand, uneven shrinkage can occur when the quilt is laundered, causing the quilt to pucker and hang poorly. Attain maximum shrinkage by washing the fabric and then drying it in a dryer. Remove it from the dryer before it is completely dry and press with a steam iron set on "wool."

Appliqué is easier than ever, thanks to many products that are available in quilt and fabric shops today. Using the proper tools and supplies gives a more accomplished result. My husband tells me, "You have to use good tools to do a good job."

THREAD

Many quiltmakers have favorite brands and types of thread. If you have a favorite, use it. As with any appliqué technique, it is important to use what you find most comfortable.

Thread is made from a variety of fibers. My favorite thread for appliqué is 100% cotton or cotton-wrapped polyester. These kinds of thread come in all colors imaginable, making it easy to match fabric colors.

Rayon thread is usually used for decorative effects as it is not as strong as cotton or polyester thread. Its sheen lends a sparkle to embroidered details.

Silk, like rayon, is very delicate and is beautiful for special effects in areas not subjected to heavy wear. Color selection is limited and it can be difficult to find.

Monofilament nylon is used more frequently in machine appliqué and it holds up well to wear. However, it imparts a stiffer feel to the quilt. Monofilament threads come in clear and smoky colors that blend well with surrounding fabrics that have highly contrasting colors and values.

For most appliqué, regular sewing-weight thread is appropriate. Some quiltmakers like the thread manufactured for fine heirloom sewing, claiming the thread draws through the fabric more smoothly. Thread that is spun and treated especially for hand quilting can be used for appliqué, although its thicker nature makes it difficult to hide the appliqué stitches.

Choose thread to match the color of the piece you are appliquéing rather than the color of the background fabric. When deciding the color that matches best, I remember an old saying I learned in 4-H, "Match your thread a little darker; you want a seam, not a marker." A lighter-value thread shows more; a darker value looks more like a shadow in the weave of the fabric, therefore is less obvious.

Sometimes a contrasting thread works well as an additional design element. In many old quilts, a buttonhole stitch done in black thread is common. The better the color match is, the less the imperfect stitches will show on your quilt.

NEEDLES

Choosing a comfortable needle is important for your success with appliqué. You may have to experiment to find the needle brands and lengths that you prefer for each appliqué task.

Two types of needles for appliqué are Sharps and Betweens. Many quiltmakers prefer Sharps for appliqué, while Betweens are favorites for quilting. With Sharps, the higher the needle number, the longer the needle length. With Betweens, the higher the needle number, the shorter the needle length.

Embroidery needles often have very large, easy-to-thread eyes, but because they are usually long and thick, they are awkward for the fine movements needed for appliqué.

When I buy needles, I check the size of the eyes. Trying to thread a small-eyed needle is frustrating and time-consuming.

NEEDLE-THREADER

Many quiltmakers find a needle-threader helpful to thread tiny needle eyes.

BEESWAX

Drawing thread across a lump of beeswax two or three times after it's been threaded on a needle helps strengthen the thread and reduces the tendency of the thread to knot during appliqué.

PINS

I use plastic bead-headed pins with long shafts that are made especially for quilting. They don't hurt your fingers when you pin for extended periods of time and don't melt if you happen to touch them with an iron.

SCISSORS

For appliqué, 3½" embroidery scissors are the most convenient. They are ideal for cutting sewing thread and snipping tightly curved areas. Thread clips are also handy.

Some quiltmakers use special appliqué scissors. These have one narrow blade and one large, blunted, semicircular blade set at an angle. They allow you to trim away excess fabric without accidentally piercing holes or cutting slices in the appliqué work.

THIMBLES

Many quiltmakers can't work without their thimbles. Others find them cumbersome and aggravating. There are many thimble types available. Experiment to discover your preference. For appliqué and general sewing purposes, I use a standard thimble, and for quilting, I use a rimmed thimble.

Some quiltmakers wear a leather thimble to protect the finger that returns the needle from the back side of the quilt to the top side. It allows the wearer to feel the tip of the needle but keeps the skin from being pierced.

A recent innovation is a thimble that has an opening at the tip for quilters with long, elegant fingernails.

To choose a thimble that fits you, try it on. Shake your hand gently. The thimble should not come off easily, but it should not be so tight that it pinches or cuts off your circulation. I own several sizes to compensate for occasional finger swelling.

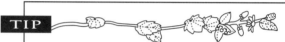

TIP

If your thimble is too large but the next size smaller is too small, gently step on the thimble to press it into a comfortable shape.

NEEDLE GRABBER

Several overlapping layers of appliqué sometimes makes it difficult for the needle to pass through the fabrics. Needle grabbers are small pieces of rubbery material that, when wrapped around the needle, help pull it through the fabric.

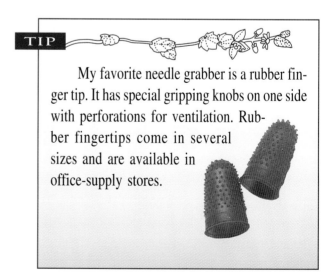

TIP

My favorite needle grabber is a rubber finger tip. It has special gripping knobs on one side with perforations for ventilation. Rubber fingertips come in several sizes and are available in office-supply stores.

TWEEZERS AND HEMOSTATS

Long-handled tweezers and hemostats make it much easier to remove paper pattern pieces after appliquéing. The tiny ends of these tools reach in where fingers can't.

Hemostats look like scissors, but instead of blades, have pincers that can be clamped shut. I use two sets: one with straight pincers and one with curved pincers. They don't lose their grip on the paper because they can be clamped shut. You can purchase hemostats at medical supply stores and some drugstores.

MARKING PENS AND PENCILS

There are several fabric marking pens and pencils on the market. Ink from blue washout pens can be rinsed out with water when the lines are no longer needed. Fadeout pens are popular but the ink is only visible for up to twenty-four hours, so you have to work quickly. These pens, along with special quilting pencils in different colors, are available in quilt shops.

Hard lead or mechanical drawing pencils also work well. My favorite marker is a white charcoal pencil that doesn't have a waxy pigment. It brushes out easily while I work and is gone by the time I finish. Look for them in art-supply stores.

To mark quilting lines, chalk, powdered chalk markers, soap slivers, and embossers all work well.

Always remember to test inks and chalks for permanence; you don't want marks to stay in the fabric forever. Even if a marking tool says it is washable, test it first on each fabric you plan to use.

REDUCING GLASS

A reducing glass is the reverse of a magnifying glass and is used to "shrink" the quilt as though you were viewing it from a distance. In a reduced format, many design problems show up that you don't see when you are up close, looking at the full size. Color, value, and balance discrepancies are accentuated in a smaller scale. Quilt shops, art-supply stores, and mail-order catalogs carry reducing glasses.

Looking through the wrong end of binoculars accomplishes the same thing. The peepholes that are installed in doors also serve the same purpose. You can buy them at hardware stores. Thread one with a ribbon and wear it around your neck.

GETTING READY

Making Appliqué Templates

When you want to cut many appliqué pieces from the same pattern, it is handy to have sturdy templates for each pattern piece. Several materials can be used for making templates, including sheets of template plastic, X-ray film, heavy paper, card stock, manila folders, and even recipe cards. Paper template materials do not hold up as well as plastic templates because the edges get distorted after repeated use. If a template will only be used a few times, paper templates are sufficient.

PLASTIC AND X-RAY FILM TEMPLATES

You can buy template plastic in quilt shops and draw directly onto it with markers. Trace the pattern onto the plastic and cut the marking line away (so that you don't enlarge the template).

It is more difficult to see a mark on X-ray film. An accurate method for transferring a pattern to X-ray film (or other plastic material) is to make a paper tracing of the pattern piece, then bond it to the template material with a glue stick. On the back of the pattern, deliberately cross the pattern's lines with the glue so that the cut edges stick to the film.

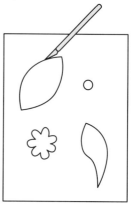

Back of pattern

Lay the glued paper pattern piece on the template material and let it dry. Then trim away the excess paper while cutting away the lines.

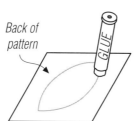

The paper-pattern piece adheres for a long time to the template material; just a touch up with glue stick will re-adhere the paper if it begins to pull away.

Mark the right side of your template piece; sometimes the pattern calls for flipping the template, and it is nice to see at a glance which side is the right side.

Making Window Templates

A set of window templates for each wreath will aid in selecting specific fabrics when you want to create dimension and depth. On an 8½" x 11" sheet of paper, carefully cut out one of each different pattern piece on the stitching line. Use a sharp razor blade or knife on your rotary-cutting mat, or use scissors to cut them out.

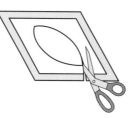

You now have a window for the shape of each different leaf, berry, or flower petal. You can fit most of the windows for each wreath on one piece of paper.

Now you can move or rotate each pattern piece's window over your fabric, searching for the perfect texture and/or colors to get the design effect for that piece.

When you have located the perfect spot, lay the corresponding pattern template in the window, remove the window template, and mark or cut out the fabric piece. Be sure to add $\frac{1}{4}$"-wide seam allowances when you cut.

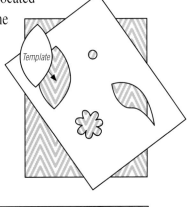

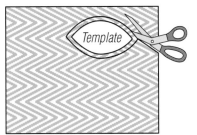

You will be amazed at the effects you can capture with window templates. Some of the most ghastly fabrics yield the most dramatic results! Especially nice are the large-scale prints with a painted quality.

Preparing the Background Block

BACKGROUND FABRIC

The blocks in this book are 15" square, finished, unless otherwise stated. I cut $16\frac{1}{2}$"–17" square blocks to compensate for the fabric "drawing up" during appliqué. After completing the appliqué, I trim the block to the required dimensions ($15\frac{1}{2}$" x $15\frac{1}{2}$").

Before you cut the background blocks, study your background fabric. Check carefully to see if there is a directional effect. This is common with prints, even those that don't appear to be directional. Some solid fabrics, due to weave structure, appear to change if rotated 90°.

To determine whether a fabric has directional characteristics, fold the fabric lengthwise (selvages together), right sides facing out. Pin the fabric lengthwise on a wall. Fold the lower left edge of the fabric up and across the fall of the fabric, forming an L. Stand away from the wall to see if there is a difference in the pattern direction where the two fabric sections meet.

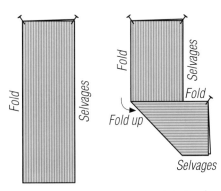

Note how light falling across a fabric sometimes makes it appear to have a different value or even a different color when it's rotated 90°. Use these wonderful subtle effects to enhance your quilt.

FABRIC GRAIN LINE

The Warp

After checking for directional patterns in the background, I study the grain line. The fabric grain is the direction of the warp (the longest threads running in the lengthwise direction of the yardage). The selvages (finished edges) run parallel to the warp. The warp is the most stable direction of the yardage; it stretches the least.

A line drawn parallel to the warp is referred to as "straight of grain" or "on grain." Hanging a fabric on grain results in the least amount of stretch. If a quilt composed of heavy fabrics and embellishments will be hung over a long period of time, grain line is an important consideration in planning the quilt.

Binding and stems cut from on-grain strips of fabrics will be stable but will not have the flexibility that is needed for smooth curves.

The Weft

The threads that run perpendicular to the warp threads and selvages are the weft. A line drawn parallel to the weft is known as "cross grain." The direction of the weft is slightly more stretchy than the warp.

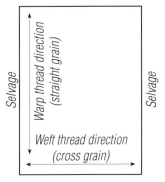

The Bias

Any line that is not on grain or cross grain is known as "bias." "True bias" is a line drawn at a 45° angle to the warp and weft. When pulled between two points along a bias line, fabric stretches, with the most stretch occurring along the true bias.

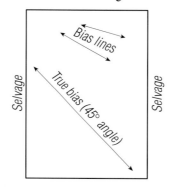

A quilt oriented on the bias should not be hung for a long period of time unless measures have been taken to prevent it from stretching. Quilting lines spaced no more than 1" apart and a backing of on-grain fabric helps stabilize a bias quilt top.

Binding and stems cut from bias strips yield the smoothest and most flexible curves.

GENERAL INSTRUCTIONS

For each of the wreaths, follow these steps for preparing the background block before you begin to appliqué.

1. For the 15" finished wreath blocks, cut your background fabric into 16½"–17" squares.
2. Fold this square into quarters. Press to mark the quadrants. With letter Z at the center of the block, align the dotted lines of the pattern along the fabric fold. Draw the quadrant, then pivot the block 90° and draw the next quadrant. Repeat until all four quadrants are drawn.

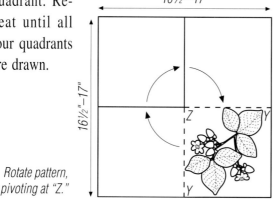

Rotate pattern, pivoting at "Z."

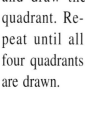
TRANSFERRING THE PATTERN TO THE BACKGROUND FABRIC

Transferring the pattern to the background fabric can be done in one of several ways. Refer to "Marking Pens and Pencils" on page 13.

Marking Directly on the Fabric Block

Some quiltmakers prefer to draw directly onto the background fabric. Use a light table or lay a piece of glass or translucent plastic between two tables (or on a table with a leaf removed), with a lamp placed underneath. A window or sliding glass door also works well.

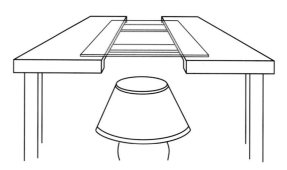

Make your own "light table."

Tape the pattern to the glass surface, then center the fabric over the pattern. Pull the fabric taut (but not enough to stretch the fabric) and tape it to the glass. Use a marking pen or pencil to transfer the pattern to the background block.

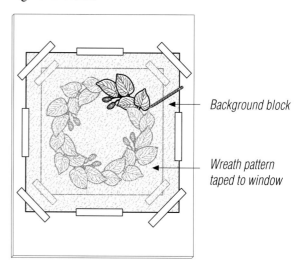

Background block

Wreath pattern taped to window

Some quiltmakers draw placement lines ⅛"–¼" inside the location where each pattern piece will go, then center the prepared appliqué pieces over the marked placement line. Because the placement lines are covered by appliqué, marking lines don't need to be washed out.

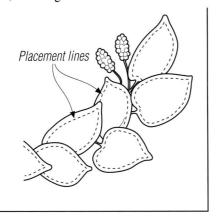

Placement lines

Preparing Templates

To make templates from the quadrant patterns, place a piece of white paper or tracing paper over the quadrant and trace around each leaf needed.

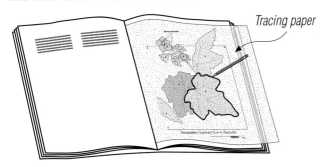

Tracing paper

If there are two or more of the same leaf (for example, leaf A), choose the leaf with the fewest overlapping leaves to make the template. Sketch an outline for any part of a leaf covered by other leaves; it will not show when overlapping leaves are appliquéd.

Cut out the template on the stitching line; do not add seam allowances. Trace around or glue this pattern to template plastic for a more permanent template.

Using Tracing Paper

If you do not wish to mark directly on your background fabric, try the technique that I prefer.

1. Using a permanent ink pen, trace a full wreath onto a large sheet of tracing paper to make a pattern.
2. Pin the pattern to the background fabric in three corners. Slide each prepared appliqué piece (stem, leaf, berry, etc.) under the tracing paper onto the background block and position it in its place on the background block, using the pattern as a guide.
3. Pin the pieces in place underneath the tracing paper. Several appliqué pieces can be placed before pinning if you are careful and don't move the other pattern pieces. Place and pin each quadrant's appliqué pieces before rotating it 90° to work on the next quadrant. Change the three corner pins holding the tracing paper in place as you rotate the wreath.

Unmarked background fabric square

Tracing paper with drawn block design

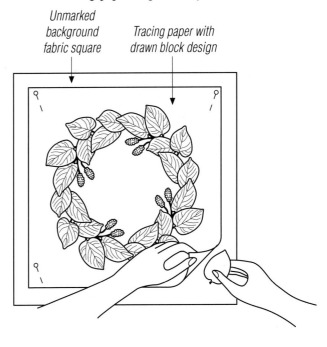

APPLIQUÉ METHODS

Preparing Appliqué Pieces

There are several different ways to prepare and appliqué the pieces for your design. Each technique has its advantages, so you can decide which work best for you. Try each method several times to gain confidence. You will find appliqué more satisfying if you have a few techniques in your "skills collection."

Making Stems

Many of the blocks in this quilt require $1/4$"-wide (finished width) stem segments. Using a standard width makes it easy to prepare several lengths of stem segments at one time and then cut them into shorter lengths as you make each block.

TO CUT BIAS STRIPS:

1. Fold one corner of a $1/2$- to 1-yard piece of fabric to its opposite corner, creating a triangle.

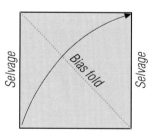

2. Cut along the fold so that the square equals two tri-angles. Use the resulting 45° edge as a guide to cut strips along the true bias.

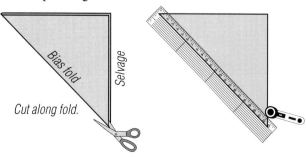

Cut along fold.

STRIP WIDTHS

I use a formula to determine the width for cutting bias strips. First, double the desired finished width of the stem segment, then add $5/8$". For example, if you need a $1/4$"-wide stem, double that measurement to $1/2$", then add $5/8$". Cut $1 1/8$"-wide bias strips.

BIAS-PRESS-BAR METHOD

An easy way to make bias tubes from bias strips of fabric is to use bias press bars or Celtic bars. These bars come in a variety of widths.

Making Bias Tubes

1. Cut the number of strips that you need for your project. If desired, sew strips, right sides together, to make one or more long strips. Press the seams open, taking care not to distort them.

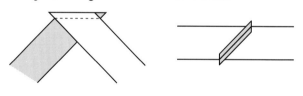

Joining Bias-Cut Strips

2. Fold the strip in half lengthwise, wrong sides together; stitch it to-gether with a $1/4$"-wide seam. From the fold (not the seam-allowance edges) to the stitching line, the dis-tance should measure the finished stem width plus one or two threads to allow room to slip the bar into the resulting tube.

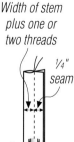

Width of stem plus one or two threads

$1/4$" seam

Fold

3. For a ¼"-wide finished stem, trim the seam allowance to ⅛" so that it will not show from the front when it's appliquéd to the block. Wider stems do not need to be trimmed except to reduce the bulk.

4. Insert the appropriate-width bias press bar into the tube and roll the seam to the underside so that the raw edges do not show when the bar is turned over.

5. Press the seam allowances to one side while pressing a crease in the fabric tube along both edges of the bar. Be careful! Metal bars get very hot. Turn the bar over and press the unseamed side of the tube.

6. Slide the tube along the bar and repeat steps 4 and 5 until the entire strip has been pressed.

7. Remove the tube from the bar and press again, on the unseamed side, to create sharp creases along both edges of the tube. The bias tubing is ready to be cut into stems.

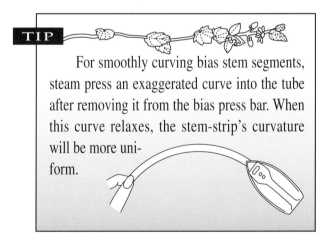

TIP

For smoothly curving bias stem segments, steam press an exaggerated curve into the tube after removing it from the bias press bar. When this curve relaxes, the stem-strip's curvature will be more uniform.

FOLDED-STRIP METHOD

Follow the directions below to make stems without using bias press bars.

1. Cut bias strips, following the directions on page 18, and follow steps 1–3 of "Making Bias Tubes," beginning on page 18.

2. Press the tube flat, creating a crease along the fold. Press the seam allowances to the back, making sure the raw edges do not show when the strip is turned to the front side.

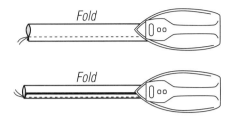
Fold

Fold

3. Press the finished tubing on the front side, being careful not to press wrinkles into the crease lines.

4. The bias tubing is ready to be cut into stems.

FLAT-STRIP METHOD

This is another method for preparing stem segments.

1. Cut bias strips, following the directions on page 18, and follow steps 1–3 of "Making Bias Tubes," beginning on page 18.

2. Press the tube flat. The stem segment is now ready to appliqué.

3. Place the seam line of the stem segment on the stem placement line as shown. The seam allowance will be within the two stem placement lines, so that when completed, the seam will not show. Stitch the stem to the background along the stem placement line.

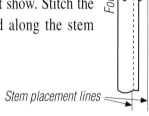
Fold

Stem placement lines

4. Fold the stem over as shown and stitch the other side of the stem to the background. The fold of the tube (stem) should cover the remaining stem placement line.

Stem placement lines

Machine Basting

Machine basting appliqué pieces to the background block makes it easier to take your work with you, and it reduces the chances that you will prick yourself on pins. Machine basting secures the pieces and helps prevent the shifting that often occurs with pinned pieces.

I prepare all of my appliqué pieces, then machine baste them to the background block. I even machine baste pieces that have been prepared by the freezer-paper-on-top method. During appliqué, I clip the basting thread, then pin a piece if it crosses exposed seam allowances that need to be turned under.

Note: This technique works best if you have a walking foot on your machine.

1. Use a long stitch length (4 stitches per inch).
2. Sharp needles work best; replace dull needles.
3. Test your fabrics to make sure needle and pinholes don't make permanent marks.
4. Pin the prepared appliqué pieces to your background fabric.

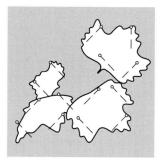

5. Machine baste the prepared pieces to the background fabric by catching each piece securely. While appliquéing, add extra pins if needed to further secure each piece until it is stitched down.

TIP

For blocks with multiple layers, machine baste the underlying pieces, then appliqué them. Repeat the same process with each layer of pieces.

Hand Appliqué

NEEDLE-TURN

This technique is probably the most efficient, since only one line must be drawn to prepare the pattern piece. I find the needle-turn method to be most useful for appliquéing small, intricate outlines. Other preparation methods reduce the sharp definition of complex shapes.

Note: Small curved pieces, such as berries, are not ideally suited for the needle-turn method. Small circles are difficult to needle-turn evenly.

1. Trace around each template on the right side of the fabric. Cut out the fabric piece, adding a scant $1/4$"-wide seam allowance ($3/16$"–$1/4$" wide) on all sides.

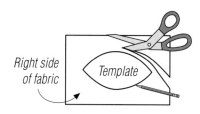

Right side of fabric · Template

2. Pin or baste the pattern piece to the background block.
3. Using the tip of your needle, carefully turn under the seam allowance just until the line disappears. Try to keep the line from disappearing too far under the piece; otherwise the overall size of the piece will "shrink" and possibly cause problems for overlapping pieces later. As you work, turn only one or two stitch lengths ahead of where your thread comes out. Resist the temptation to turn under and finger-press more than this unless you are turning under long, straight areas.

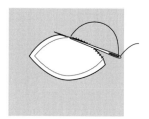

TIP

- Begin appliqué on the straightest portion of the pattern piece.
- To get smoothly curved edges, clip inside curves along seam allowances before turning. Clip up to, but not across, the stitching line. Clip only until the curve is smooth. If your fabric is loosely woven, make fewer clips so the fabric will not fray during appliqué.

Clip

PAPER PIECING

Many quiltmakers prefer the paper-pieced method of appliqué preparation because the turned and basted edges become crisp, making them easier to work with. Most pattern pieces can be paper-pieced, although complex shapes are more difficult to baste.

Several paper products are used for paper piecing. White construction paper is favored by many quiltmakers. Others find the advertising "pullouts" in magazines to be the right weight. Use this paper cautiously because the ink sometimes rubs off onto the fabric or fingers.

New to the paper-piecing scene is "wall liner." This heavy, fibrous paper is typically used to smooth walls before covering them with wallpaper. It doesn't have glue or other adhesives on it, and its heavier weight makes it ideal for appliqué. It gives a wonderfully firm edge to appliqué against, yet yields to the needle during basting; if you accidentally catch wall liner with your thread during appliqué, you can easily pull away the wall liner. It is my favorite for paper-piecing berries, seeds, or grapes. Wall liner is sold by the roll and can be purchased where wallpaper is sold.

Note: Because the gasses in wood-fiber paper burn fabric over the years, remove all paper from the quilt. If you wish to leave the paper in the quilt for shaping, use 100% rag paper, available in art supply stores.

To paper-piece:

1. Trace around the template onto one of the papers mentioned above. Do not add seam allowances to the paper pieces.
2. Cut out the paper piece along the seam line. Mark the right side of the paper piece.

Paper
Template
Seam line

3. Cut out your fabric piece, adding a scant $1/4$"-wide seam allowance. If you want to achieve a special effect, remember to place the template on the fabric accordingly. (See pages 14–15.)
4. Place the paper piece on the back side of the fabric, being careful not to reverse the pattern. Turn under the seam allowances and baste around the fabric piece, remembering to clip inside curves and corners if necessary.

Paper piece
Back side of fabric
Basting stitches

5. To turn outside points, fold the tip of the point perpendicular to the point as shown.

Fold
Paper piece
Fabric

6. Fold the seam allowances over the paper and baste between the points.

Paper piece

7. To turn under the seams of inside points, clip the fabric piece to within two or three threads of the paper's edge. Fold over the seam allowance as shown and baste.

Clip
Back side of fabric
Paper piece
Paper piece

8. Pin or baste the prepared piece in place on the background block and appliqué to within ¹/₂" to 1" from the starting point.
9. Pull out the basting thread and remove the paper.
10. Appliqué the remaining portion of the piece.

 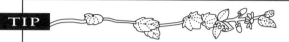
Paper-Piecing Small Pieces

Smooth edges are easy when you paper-piece small round or oval pieces, such as berries or seedpods. Wall liner is my favorite method for paper-piecing these small shapes.

1. Prepare the paper pattern and fabric piece as described in steps 1–3 on page 21.
2. Starting on the right side of the fabric, do a running stitch around the perimeter of the fabric piece about ¹/₈" from the edge of the fabric. Keep your stitches about ¹/₈" long so that the fabric gathers evenly around the pattern piece. End your line of basting on the right side of the fabric.

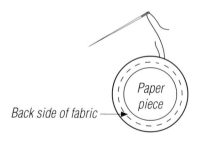

Back side of fabric → Paper piece

3. Gently pull the ends of the basting thread to gather the fabric around the paper piece. Be careful not to bend the paper inside the fabric. Knot and trim the thread ends.

Paper piece

4. Press, if needed, then pin or baste in place on the background fabric. Appliqué in place.
5. Turn the block over and make a tiny cut through the background fabric to make an opening. Don't cut through to the front! Use tweezers or a hemostat to carefully pull out the paper pattern.
6. Stitch the cut closed with a few whipstitches, being careful not to pull or pucker the background fabric.

FREEZER PAPER

Freezer paper has long been a favorite for paper piecing. It has a shiny, coated side and an uncoated side. When heated with a dry, hot iron, the coated side softens slightly and adheres to fabric. It pulls away easily when it is no longer needed. Find freezer paper in the food preservation section of your favorite grocery store.

Freezer Paper on Top

This method is essentially the same as needle-turn appliqué except that a freezer-paper template is used instead of drawing a line directly onto the appliqué piece. It is an excellent method to use for intricately shaped pieces. Noted quilt designer Elly Sienkiewicz prefers this method for her beautiful (and intricate) Baltimore Album quilts.

1. With the *right side of the template facing up*, trace the pattern onto the *uncoated* side of the freezer paper. Cut it out on the traced line (seam line); do not add seam allowances to the freezer-paper pattern piece.

2. Place the *coated* side of the freezer-paper pattern on the right side of the fabric. Press the freezer paper to the fabric for about three seconds, using a dry iron (no steam or spray, on the "wool" setting). Experiment with this until you find what works best.

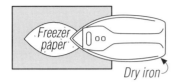

Freezer paper

Dry iron

It is sometimes difficult to remove freezer paper from shiny fabrics or those with a glazed finish. On these fabrics, just touch the iron to the freezer paper so that it doesn't form a strong bond. Test on a scrap, letting the paper and fabric cool completely before attempting to remove the paper. If you still have difficulty removing the paper, try warming it with the iron, then pulling it off before it has cooled.

3. Cut out the fabric piece, adding a scant ¼"-wide seam allowance. Clip all of the inside curves so that they will lie flat when turned.

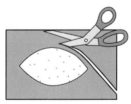

4. With the tip of the needle, turn under the seam allowance so that it is completely under the edge of the freezer paper. The edge of the freezer paper is the stitching guide.

5. When the piece has been appliquéd, gently pull off the freezer paper. The freezer-paper piece may be reused if it isn't too fuzzy.

Paper-Pieced Freezer Paper

This method of adhering freezer paper to the back of an appliqué piece ensures a secure placement during the basting process.

1. With the *wrong side of the template facing up,* trace the pattern onto the *uncoated* side of the freezer paper. Cut on the traced line (seam line); do not add seam allowances to the freezer-paper pattern.

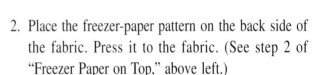

Template (wrong side up)

Freezer paper

2. Place the freezer-paper pattern on the back side of the fabric. Press it to the fabric. (See step 2 of "Freezer Paper on Top," above left.)
3. Cut out the fabric appliqué piece, adding a scant ¼"-wide seam allowance.
4. Hand baste the seam allowances to the back of the appliqué piece.

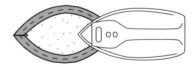

Freezer paper

5. On the back side of the piece, gently press the basted seam allowances to create smooth, even curves.

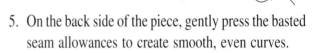

6. Pin or baste the prepared piece in place on the background block. Appliqué to within ½"–1" from the starting point.
7. Pull out the basting thread and remove the paper piece. Finish appliquéing.

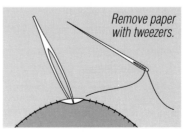

Remove paper with tweezers.

Press-Basted Freezer Paper

This method of freezer-paper preparation eliminates the need for hand basting.

1. With the *right side of the template facing up,* trace the pattern onto the *uncoated* side of the freezer paper.

2. Cut out the freezer-paper pattern on the traced line (seam line); *do not add seam allowances* to the freezer-paper pattern.

3. Cut out the fabric piece, adding a scant ¼"-wide seam allowance. Clip all inside curves so that they will lie flat when turned.

4. Place the uncoated side of the freezer-paper piece on the back side of the fabric. The shiny side will face up.

Shiny side of freezer paper —

Back side of fabric —

5. With the iron tip, fold the seam allowance over the shiny side of the freezer paper to bond it in place.

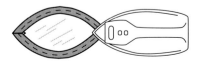

6. Pin or baste the prepared piece in place on the background block. Appliqué to within ½"–1" from the starting point.

7. Remove the paper piece and finish appliquéing.

INTERFACED APPLIQUÉ

This is one of my favorite techniques. It requires a little time at the sewing machine, but the results are well worth the extra step.

Interfaced appliqué is great for large, straight or gently curving pieces. This technique does not work well for intricate designs and small, pointed or notched areas.

Use the lightest-weight *nonfusible* interfacing you can find. My favorite weight is specified for sheer to lightweight fabrics. Do not use fusible interfacing as it will ruin your cut pieces.

1. With the template facing right side up, trace the pattern (along the seam line) onto the nonfusible, lightweight interfacing, using a blue washout marking pen. Cut it out, adding ¼"-wide seam allowances.

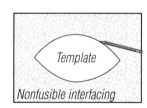

Template

Nonfusible interfacing

2. Stitch the nonfusible interfacing to the right side of the fabric piece, using a small stitch length (12–14 stitches per inch). Stitch about a thread's width to the outside of the drawn seam line. This prevents the piece from "shrinking" when it's turned right side out.

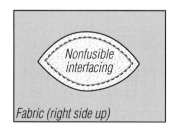

Nonfusible interfacing

Fabric (right side up)

3. Carefully trim the seam allowances with pinking shears. Do not cut into the stitching.

TIP

Trimming the edges with pinking shears is usually sufficient; however, inside curves occasionally need a little more clipping.

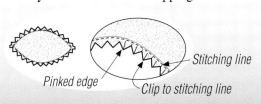

Pinked edge

Clip to stitching line

Stitching line

4. Cut an opening in the interfacing to within ¹/₂" of the stitching.

5. Turn the piece right side out; the interfacing creates a "facing" for the appliqué piece.

6. Spray the interfaced side with water to remove the blue lines. Blot the excess moisture, then press the facing so it doesn't show from the right side. You should have a perfectly turned piece, ready to appliqué.

TIP

To remove the blue lines, immerse the pieces in a dishpan of water until they are saturated, then lay them on an old white terry cloth towel, interfaced side up, and roll up the towel tightly. When you unroll the towel, you can see the pieces that still bleed. Rinse again until they blot clear.

7. Machine or hand baste the interfaced pieces in place, then appliqué. Refer to "Machine Basting" on page 20.

8. If you have used a lightweight interfacing, there is no need to cut it away from the back. It is easy to quilt through both layers.

Reverse Appliqué

Molas, folk-art panels stitched into blouses by the Cuna women of the San Blas Islands in Panama, have elevated reverse appliqué to celebrity status. Areas of reverse appliqué, from large openings to tiny slits, are made by cutting, turning under, and stitching the top layer of fabric, revealing the color beneath. Stack several layers of fabric, then cut through and appliqué each, one by one, revealing color after color in concentric openings.

To make a two-color section:

1. Begin with two layers of fabric, pinned or basted together. Draw the stitching line with the marking tool of your choice, then cut or slash *only* the top layer of fabric.

2. Turn the cut edges under, exposing the lower layer of fabric. Appliqué the top layer to the layer below it, using the blind stitch. Clip where necessary to get a smooth edge. The thread color should match the top layer.

For slits

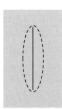  

For larger openings

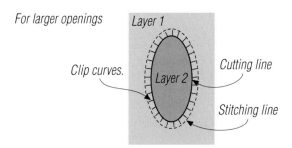

Layer 1

Clip curves.

Layer 2

Cutting line

Stitching line

To make a section with more than two colors:

1. Cut an opening in the uppermost layer, remembering to allow a scant ¹/₄"-wide seam allowance.

2. Turn the edges under and appliqué, clipping curves where necessary to get a smooth edge.

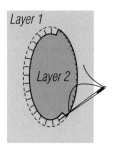

Layer 1

Layer 2

3. Cut a smaller opening in the next layer and appliqué to the layer below.

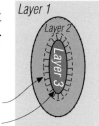

Layer 1

Layer 2

Layer 3

New stitching line (second layer)
New cutting line (second layer)

4. Continue cutting and stitching, one layer at a time, until the bottom layer is revealed. Do not cut the lowest layer.

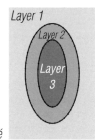

Layer 1

Layer 2

Layer 3

Finished Reverse Appliqué

Note: This technique works best with 100% cotton fabrics. Turning under the narrow seam allowances in small openings is difficult with synthetic blends.

Hand-Appliqué Stitches

Your appliqué pieces are prepared and in place on the background block. Now it's time to thread that needle and get to work!

THREADING THE NEEDLE

To reduce thread torque, which causes annoying knots to form during stitching, follow these steps:

1. Before you cut the thread off the spool, cut the end of the thread, creating a clean, even edge that will go through a needle eye more easily. Cutting thread at an angle instead of straight across sometimes makes it easier to thread.

2. The proper way to unwind thread from the spool is to hold the spool loosely at the top and bottom and pull from the side.

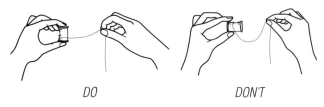

DO   *DON'T*

3. Instead of trying to push the thread through the needle, try "needling the thread" or pushing the needle eye over the end of the thread.

TIP

❧ If you have trouble threading the needle, lick the needle eye before pushing it over the thread end. The saliva acts as a lubricant, drawing the thread through the eye more easily.

❧ Waxing, then flattening, the end of the thread between a thumb and finger helps to thread a stubborn needle as well. Recut the end of the thread to get a "sharper" end.

❧ If the needle still won't be threaded, try turning the needle over. The eye is punched from one side during manufacture, which sometimes creates a side that is more easily threaded.

4. Pull the thread through the eye, then pull 18" of thread off the spool and cut. Wax the thread at this point, if desired (see below), and knot the newly cut end.

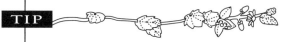

TIP

❧ For left-handed quiltmakers, reverse the order; knot the end you put through the needle, then cut the thread from the spool. My left-handed students notice a difference when they follow this tip.

❧ Many quiltmakers find a needle-threader helpful to thread hard-to-see needle eyes.

WAXING THE THREAD

Waxing the thread helps reduce its tendency to knot. Try stitching without beeswax, then wax the thread and continue stitching. You'll become a believer!

1. Thread the needle. Cut the thread but do not knot it. Hold the needle in one hand and the lump of beeswax in the fingers of your other hand.

2. At the needle eye, place the thread on top of the beeswax and place your other thumb lightly on top of the thread.

3. Exerting gentle pressure with your thumb, slowly draw the thread over the beeswax two or three times. Be careful! If you pull the thread too fast or with too much pressure, the thread can burn or cut your thumb.

Usually a thread only needs to be drawn through beeswax at the beginning of its use; however, some threads knot more frequently than others. Rewaxing such thread once or twice during its use seems to help.

If you find beeswax leaves a slight stain on your fabric, try using paraffin instead. Test a waxed thread on a sample of your fabric before appliquéing your project.

STITCHING

There are two ways of orienting your work as you appliqué. One is to work so that the stitching runs along the upper edge and the body of the appliqué piece is below the needle. The other way is to appliqué along the lower edge of the piece.

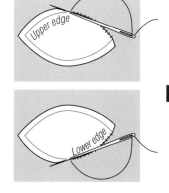

The illustrations for appliqué in this book show the method of appliquéing along the upper edge of the piece. It is the method most appliqué books use to illustrate the appliqué stitch.

My preference is to appliqué along the lower edge. I can see the background fabric and the folded edge this way. I also find it is easier during needle-turn to be able to see the exact point where the line turns under and where the fold should begin. Try both methods to discover your preference.

BLIND STITCH

The most common stitch used for appliqué is the blind stitch. If you are new to appliqué, practice with this stitch.

1. Pin or baste the appliqué piece in place. Begin stitching by burying the knot inside the turned edge or start on the back side of the background fabric. Bring the needle up through the background fabric and into the piece you are appliquéing, catching two or three threads of its folded edge. Do not run the needle along the inside of the turned edge before bringing it out.

2. Return the needle to the background fabric right next to the point where the thread came out of the appliqué piece. Move the needle ahead $1/8$", then bring it up through the background fabric and catch just two or three threads of the appliqué piece's turned edge. Try to make your stitches as invisible as possible from the top.

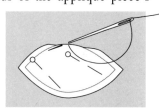

TIP

Stitches should be no farther than $1/8$" apart. Larger stitch intervals can cause problems if the stitch is cut accidently. For example, if the stitches are $1/4$" apart, one cut stitch will leave a $1/2$" gap between the two stitches on either side of the cut stitch. A gap can be snagged easily and the appliqué pulled out.

From the back side, your stitches should appear as tiny diagonal lines outlining the shape of the appliquéd piece.

ENDING THE STITCHING LINE

When you finish appliquéing a piece, turn the block over. On the back side, take two tiny stitches on top of each other at the end of the just completed stitches.

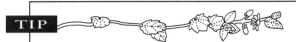
APPLIQUÉING NOTCHES

Notches or inside points are found frequently in appliqué. Hearts are a favorite motif and each heart has a notch. Practice will help you perfect this technique.

1. At the notch, clip the seam allowance to within one or two threads of the turning line. Turn the seam allowance under (unless you have already basted it under) and stitch to within one stitch of the notch.

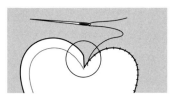

2. After the seam allowances are turned under on both sides of the notch, set your needle into the background fabric at the point of the notch but a little deeper under the appliqué piece.
3. Bring the needle back up through the appliqué piece and to one side of the notch, taking a deeper stitch than usual (i.e., take a scant $1/16$" "bite" rather than bringing the needle out right at the fold).

4. Set your needle into the background fabric in the same place as the previous stitches and bring it up directly above the notch, again taking an extra bite into the appliqué piece. By including this extra fabric in the stitches and by putting the needle into the background a little farther under the appliqué piece, the turned edges of the seam allowance will roll a little, securing any loose threads that result from the clips that you made in step 1.

5. Put the needle into the same background point again. Bring the needle out to the other side of the notch, taking an extra bite into the turned edge. Return the needle to the same background spot under the notch. You have made a tiny crow's foot at the notch. Finish appliquéing the piece.

Practice appliquéing a few notches before beginning your project.

HAND BUTTONHOLE-STITCH APPLIQUÉ

For an old-fashioned look, secure the edges of the appliqué pieces with a buttonhole stitch. Traditionally, black thread was used for the buttonhole stitch; contrasting colors give a more updated look.

Prepare your pieces as you would for the needle-turn or interfaced appliqué technique. Stitch a continuous line just outside the edge of the appliqué piece, with the perpendicular lines penetrating both the appliqué piece and the background fabric.

Refer to "Embroidery Stitches" on pages 33–34 for buttonhole-stitch instructions.

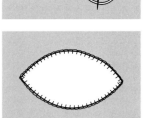

Machine Appliqué and Stitches

Lovely results are possible with machine appliqué, using one of the methods below. In addition to being beautiful, machine-appliquéd quilts are very durable. What may be sacrificed in delicacy of appearance will be gained in strength.

TIP

- ❧ Keep your machine well oiled and free of dust. If you are having trouble with thread tension and the usual adjustments don't work, clean and oil your machine.
- ❧ An open-toe appliqué foot gives an unobstructed view of the appliqué edge. It also has a smooth, indented area under the foot that allows the appliqué stitching to pass smoothly under the foot. You can use a walking foot for appliqués to prevent distorting and shifting the pieces, but it does not have the open-toe feature.

Open-toe appliqué foot

Walking foot

MACHINE SATIN-STITCH APPLIQUÉ

1. Cut the appliqué pieces from your fabrics, leaving a $\frac{1}{8}$"-wide seam allowance all around.
2. Pin or baste the pattern piece in place on the background block.

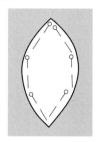

3. Stitch along the seam line, using either a straight stitch or a narrow zigzag stitch.

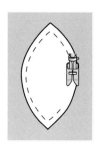

4. Trim the seam allowances to within a few threads of the stitches.

5. Select the stitch width and length. The stitch width should cover the straight stitching and the cut edges of the pattern piece. The stitch length should create a smooth, uninterrupted line without making a bulky ridge. Stitches set too closely may build up, causing the presser foot to catch on the stitching. Experiment to find the line weight and quality that looks best with your fabrics and colors.

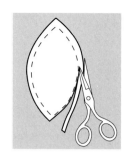

TIP

Make a sample to test the stitch. If you see tiny bobbin threads at the edges of the stitching line, thread the bobbin thread through the eye in the bobbin-case finger if your bobbin has one. Then experiment with the tension to achieve a smooth stitching line.

Thread through extra eye.

6. Begin stitching in an unobtrusive place, preferably one that will be covered later by stitching or other pattern pieces. Otherwise, if there is no overlap, begin stitching on a straight length of appliqué. It is easier to end the stitching along a straight line than on a curve.

MACHINE BUTTONHOLE-STITCH APPLIQUÉ

If your machine is equipped with a buttonhole stitch, you can achieve an old-fashioned look for your quilt. Many antique quilts have buttonhole stitching done with black thread.

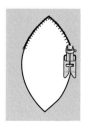

MACHINE BLIND-STITCH APPLIQUÉ

This method of appliqué gives a hand-turned look with the speed of machine work.

1. Prepare your appliqué pieces, using the paper-pieced, freezer-paper method or interfaced method.
2. Pin or baste pieces in place on background block.

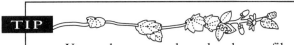

TIP

Use a clear or smoky-colored monofilament nylon thread because it will blend with the colors of the pattern piece and background fabrics.

3. Set the stitch length very short and the stitch width to take a narrow "bite." Do a few practice pieces first to establish the proper settings for your machine and fabrics.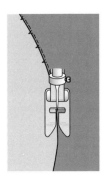

4. Blindstitch the piece in place, stopping ½" from the end to remove the paper piece. Then complete the stitching. An alternative is to stitch all the way around the piece, then make a small cut in the background, behind the piece, and remove the paper. (See "Trimming Fabric on the Back Side," below right, for details.)

Fusible-Web Appliqué

Using a fusible web with a hot iron to fuse fabric pattern pieces to a background is a quick-and-easy way to appliqué complex designs. Impressive results occur without the time investment required by traditional appliqué methods. One drawback to using fusible web is that it is difficult to hand embroider through it. Instead, machine embroider or add details with permanent drawing pens.

The medallion wreath on page 30 was created using fusible web and machine appliqué. Stitching must be used to hold down the fused edges of the appliqué pieces because they tend to peel up over time.

1. Follow the manufacturer's directions to fuse the web to the appliqué fabrics.
2. Place the fused fabric so the paper backing is facing up. With the wrong side of the template facing up, trace around the template with a pencil on the stitching line.

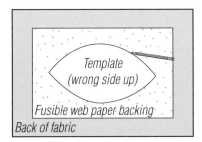

Template (wrong side up)

Fusible web paper backing

Back of fabric

3. Cut the traced pieces along the line, making sure the edges are smooth. Do not add seam allowances.
4. Carefully peel the paper backing away from the fabric appliqué piece.

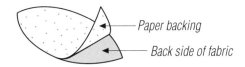

Paper backing

Back side of fabric

5. Follow the manufacturer's directions to fuse the appliqué pieces in place on the background block.
6. Use a zigzag stitch, satin stitch, or buttonhole stitch to appliqué the pieces in place. Instructions for machine-appliqué techniques begin on page 29.

Note: Since the appliquéd pieces are fused, you will not be able to cut away the background fabric.

Trimming Fabric on the Back Side

After all appliqué on a block is completed, cut away the background fabric that lies under each appliquéd piece. This reduces the bulk created by the layers of fabric and makes it easier to quilt.

Turn the block over and gently pull up on the background fabric to separate it from the appliquéd piece. Make a tiny cut in the background fabric and insert a point of your scissors.

Background fabric

Trim the fabric ¼" away from the stitching line, being careful not to cut through the appliquéd piece.

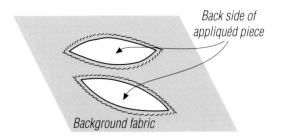

Back side of appliquéd piece

Background fabric

TIP

If you have several overlapping layers of fabric in addition to the background fabric, consider trimming away the excess layers of appliqué. Make sure your stitches are small in these pieces so they won't pull out. Restitch the pieces to secure them if necessary.

EMBROIDERED DETAILS

Embroidery Supplies and Techniques

EMBROIDERY FLOSS

When we think of embroidery floss, many of us picture six-strand skeins found in a multitude of colors. There are several brands available, and colors vary from company to company; therefore, there is a huge array of colors from which to choose. Several types of floss or thread can be used in embroidery. Try different types and combinations to find the ones that enhance your project.

Most embroidery floss is colorfast, but if you're concerned about color bleeding, rinse the skein of floss before use. Remember, as with all threads, too much handling alters the twist and sheen, making it difficult to pull it from the skein.

Strands of floss can be separated from the skein and used individually or in combination with other colors or values of the same color to get a soft, heathery look. I usually use two strands to get a flat, delicate look that also covers an area quickly. For a thicker line, I embroider two rows of stitching. The more strands of floss you use, the bulkier and more textured the look will be.

EMBROIDERY HOOPS

Embroidery hoops come in many sizes; choose the size most comfortable for your hands and the size of your work. A 6" hoop is a good, all-purpose size and is useful for many projects.

Hoops are made of plastic, steel, and wood. Wooden hoops should be smooth and splinter-free. The best hoops have a screw fastener that allows the hoop to be adjusted for different fabric weights or thicknesses.

EMBROIDERY NEEDLES

Embroidery needles come in different sizes and lengths. They usually have large eyes to accommodate more than one strand of floss. I prefer a longer needle for embroidery than I do for appliqué.

Threading the Needle

1. Carefully pull the end (the "original end") of the floss from the skein. Cut a length of about 18".

| TIP |

❦ Most of the embroidered stems in the wreath blocks are composed of three rows of stem stitch. (See page 33.) For a rounded, dimensional look to the stems, choose three values, grading from light to medium to dark. Embroider a row of each value side by side.

❦ To give berries the illusion of shine (reflection of light), make a tiny row of stem

stitches, using a very pale color. The tiny line curves with the contour of the berry.

Sometimes a French knot in a pale color is enough to achieve this effect. Use no more than two strands of floss or the knot will be too bulky.

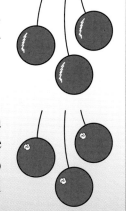

2. Hold the *original end* while you separate and pull out the desired number of strands. Pull them out, one at a time. This method "fluffs" each strand.

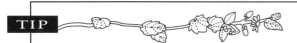

TIP

    I put the original end of each strand in my mouth after I have pulled it out of the group. Then I know which end should be put through the needle.

3. Knot the strands together at the ends that have just been cut from the skein.
4. Trim the unknotted ends, then thread the needle. (See tip above.)

TIP

    To avoid that clump of leftover strands of embroidery floss that seems to grow uncontrollably, try the following techniques:

1. Tie a slip knot at the just-cut end of the remaining 18" long strands. The slip knot marks the ends that will be knotted for use later; it releases easily, so you can pull out the strands as you need them. (To release the slip knot, pull the shorter end.)

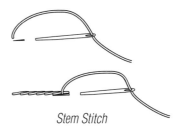

Pull this end to release slip knot.

2. Fold the strands in half, then in half again.

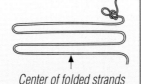

Center of folded strands

3. Hold the center of the folded strands and loop it through one loop of the original skein. Pull the ends through and gently tighten until it is snug on the skein loop. This will keep the colors matched and more lengths ready for use.

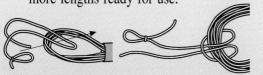

Embroidery Stitches

    The following embroidery stitches are used in the wreath blocks and borders in this book. These stitches, along with your imagination, should provide many options for you to create your own work of art. For other stitches or special effects, consult a book on embroidery stitches.

STEM STITCH

    The stem stitch is used to outline motifs or to create smooth lines of embroidery. Leaf stems, veins, and highlights are enhanced by this stitch.

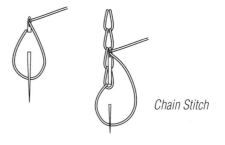

Stem Stitch

CHAIN STITCH

    This stitch may also be used for stems and outlines. Varying the stitch length and the number of floss strands yields many textural and special effects. To quickly fill in an area, chain stitch several rows next to each other.

Chain Stitch

BUTTONHOLE STITCH

    Use this stitch to make a "feathery" line of embroidery around the appliqué piece. Depending on the effect you want, use thread in a contrasting color or in a shade that complements the piece.

Buttonhole Stitch

 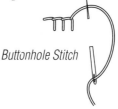

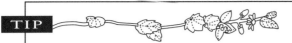

Vary the length of the perpendicular stitch and vary the width of the outline stitch, to create many different effects, including a scalloped row of stitches.

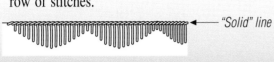

← "Solid" line

SATIN STITCH

This is an ideal stitch for covering large and small areas. Its smooth, almost shiny, effect is visually inviting, and no one can resist touching it!

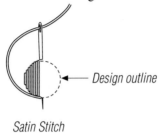

← Design outline

Satin Stitch

If the satin-stitched outline looks a bit ragged, consider embroidering a row of stem stitches around the satin-stitched area. Some embroiderers like to outline the shape first with a stem-stitch row, then satin-stitch over the line of stem stitches for a smoother shape.

FRENCH KNOT

These little gems add wonderful texture to any embroidered work. By wrapping only one thread once around the needle, you can create tiny and delicate stitches. To make big, nubby French knots, use three or more strands of floss and wrap them around the needle several times. With a little practice, they are easy and fun to make. Their appearance invites admiring fingers.

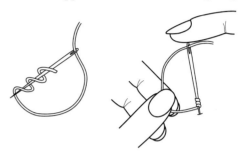

The key to making French knots look nice and not like big blobs is to hold the embroidery floss taut next to where it will return to the back side of the fabric. Then, release the floss when there is only about $3/4$" left to pull through. If you don't keep it taut, the floss twists, and unwanted extra knots are more likely to form.

BEGINNING YOUR WREATH PROJECT

Words of Encouragement

For those of you just learning to appliqué, these blocks will bear with grace any minor flaws associated with a beginner's stitches. In nature, no two leaves are identical, so there is no pressure here for perfection!

The ideas and versatility of the patterns presented in this book will keep the appliqué lover busy creating beautiful works of art. The accolades you receive will provide incentive for making many wonderful projects.

Using the Wreath Patterns

The patterns in this book are printed full size. Each wreath pattern is presented in a quadrant format. To make a complete wreath block, rotate the quadrant around the center point four times.

To make different sizes, reduce or enlarge the patterns. They have been reduced up to 50% with stunning results. (See Nancy Chong's quilt on page 50.) Remember, if you change the size of the block, the yardage requirements will change as well.

Some of the blocks are easier than others, either technically or in terms of time needed to complete them. Each wreath block is graded as to the level of difficulty:

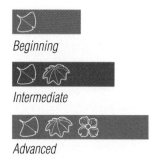

Beginning

Intermediate

Advanced

My block-of-the-month classes begin with the Salal block, as it is fairly easy for beginners. This block is great for learning many appliqué techniques.

Each pattern suggests embroidery details for completing the block. These are guidelines if you wish to embroider your wreaths. Options to replace embroidery include using permanent pens or fabric paints to emphasize details. If you do not wish to appliqué narrow leaf ends (the portion of the leaf that attaches to the stem), then embroider them instead.

Before you prepare a block for appliqué, refer to "Preparing the Background Block" on pages 15–17.

Appliqué Order

The pattern instructions provide a recommended order in which the pieces should be appliquéd. Each different leaf, flower, or berry pattern piece is assigned a letter. If the pattern piece appears more than once in the quadrant, it will be assigned a letter and a number. The number indicates the order in which the leaf is to be appliquéd. For example, leaf A1 should be appliquéd before leaf A2 and A3. Read through the directions for each wreath quadrant before you begin to appliqué.

Leaf, stem, flower, and berry placements are indicated. Appliqué the underlying pieces first, noting where they will be overlapped. Remember, you do not need to appliqué an area that will be overlapped by another piece.

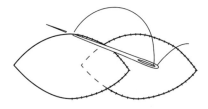

Some of the patterns have special hints or creative options for the wreath. Be innovative and use these hints and options elsewhere in your quilt.

Materials and Yardage Requirements

MATERIALS: 44"-WIDE FABRIC

Fabrics for background blocks and borders (See "Yardage Requirements," below.)

3–5 yds. total of assorted fabrics for leaves
$1^1/_2$ yds. total of assorted fabrics for flowers and berries
1 yd. total of assorted fabrics for stems
Assorted colors of embroidery floss

YARDAGE REQUIREMENTS

The following yardage requirements are *generous estimates* of what you will need for your quilt. Yardage is based on a 42" fabric width, allowing for size discrepancies and shrinkage.

Yardage Requirements for 15" Background Blocks Only *(no borders included)*

No. of Squares	2	4	6	8	10	12	18	20
Yardage Needed	$^1/_2$ yd.	1 yd.	$1^1/_2$ yds.	2 yds.	$2^1/_2$ yds.	3 yds.	$4^1/_2$ yds.	5 yds.

Yardage Requirements to Finish Quilts with 6"-Wide Border

Yardage is calculated for unseamed outer borders cut on the lengthwise grain of fabric. Cut $1^1/_2$"-wide finished inner borders from selvage to selvage. Finished size includes inner and outer borders. After cutting the outer border strips, you should have enough remaining fabric for binding. For contrasting binding, refer to the yardage chart below.

No. of Blocks along Border	Finished Size	Inner Border	Outer Border	Backing	Contrasting Binding
3 x 3	60" x 60"	$^3/_8$ yd.	2 yds.	$3^3/_4$ yds.	$^1/_2$ yd.
3 x 4	60" x 75"	$^1/_2$ yd.	$2^1/_2$ yds.	$3^3/_4$ yds.	$^1/_2$ yd.
4 x 4	75" x 75"	$^1/_2$ yd.	$2^3/_8$ yds.	$4^5/_8$ yds.	$^5/_8$ yd.
3 x 5	60" x 90"	$^1/_2$ yd.	$2^7/_8$ yds.	$5^1/_2$ yds.	$^5/_8$ yd.
4 x 5	75" x 90"	$^5/_8$ yd.	$2^7/_8$ yds.	$5^1/_2$ yds.	$^2/_3$ yd.
5 x 5	90" x 90"	$^5/_8$ yd.	$2^7/_8$ yds.	8 yds.	$^2/_3$ yd.

Yardage Requirements to Finish Quilts with 12"-Wide Border

Yardage is calculated for unseamed borders cut on the lengthwise grain of fabric. Cut 1½"-wide inner borders from selvage to selvage. Finished size includes inner and outer borders. After cutting the outer border strips, you should have enough remaining fabric for binding. For contrasting binding, refer to the yardage chart below.

No. of Blocks along Border	Finished Size	Inner Border	Outer Border	Backing	Contrasting Binding
3 x 3	72" x 72"	⅜ yd.	4½ yds.	4½ yds.	½ yd.
3 x 4	72" x 87"	⅜ yd.	4⅞ yds.	5⅜ yds.	⅝ yd.
4 x 4	87" x 87"	⅜ yd.	5¼ yds.	7¾ yds.	⅔ yd.
3 x 5	72" x 102"	½ yd.	5½ yds.	6 yds.	⅔ yd.
4 x 5	87" x 102"	½ yd.	5¾ yds.	7¾ yds.	¾ yd.
5 x 5	102" x 102"	½ yd.	6¼ yds.	9 yds.	¾ yd.

Yardage Requirements for Medallion Quilts with 12"-Wide Border

Yardage is calculated for an unseamed 12"-wide outer border cut on the lengthwise grain of fabric. Finished size includes a 1"-wide inner border between the block and outer border.

30" Medallion with 12"-Wide Outer Border	Finished Size	Background and Outer Border	Inner Border	Backing	Contrasting Binding
	56" x 56"	4¾ yds.	⅜ yd.	3½ yds.	½ yd.

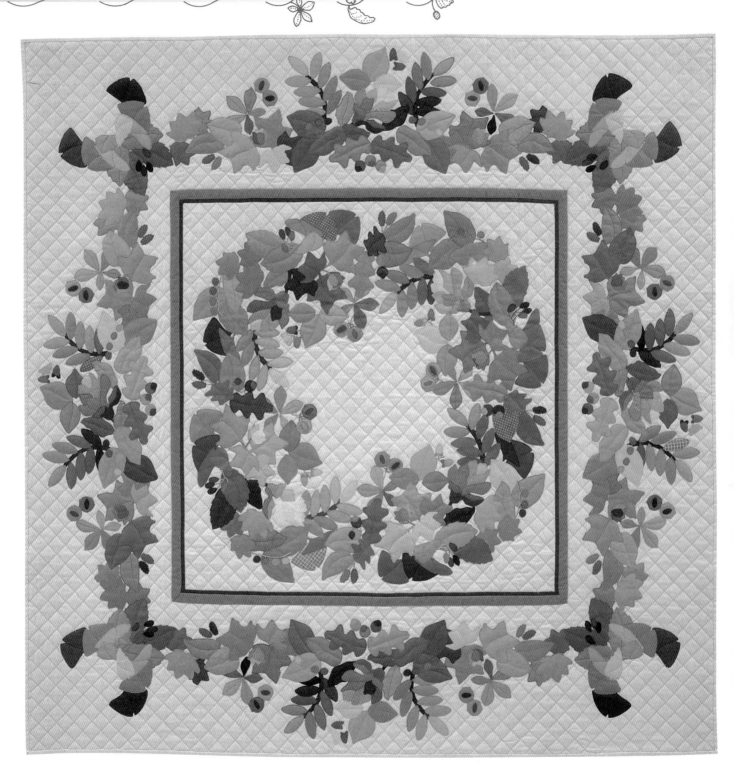

Magnolia Medallion *by Laura Munson Reinstatler, 1993, Mill Creek, Washington, 54¹/₂" x 54¹/₂".*
Pink and lavender flowers and berries complement an unusual color palette of greens and browns.
This quilt was appliquéd using the fusible-web appliqué method and machine quilted.

Bonsai Wreaths *by Nancy Lee Chong, 1993, Bellevue, Washington, 63" x 63".*
Unbelievably tiny leaves, flowers, and berries adorn this truly awe-inspiring miniature quilt. Sixteen half-size wreath blocks surround the half-size medallion wreath, providing a showcase for Nancy's extraordinary skills as a quilt artist.

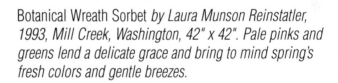

Botanical Wreath Sorbet *by Laura Munson Reinstatler, 1993, Mill Creek, Washington, 42" x 42". Pale pinks and greens lend a delicate grace and bring to mind spring's fresh colors and gentle breezes.*

Salal Soliloquy *by Laura Munson Reinstatler, 1993, Mill Creek, Washington, 32" x 32". Dainty calico prints create an old-fashioned feeling reminiscent of tea parties, dimity, and lace. Mirror images of the quadrants that form the center wreath are echoed in the border.*

Magnolia Florabunda *by Laura Munson Reinstatler, Mill Creek, Washington, 78¹/₂" x 86¹/₂". (Before appliqué, left; after appliqué, below.) This Trip Around the World is a beautiful wash of florals, ranging in color from white to navy. The palest prints have very little texture compared with the rich texture of the darker range of florals. Mirror images of Magnolia quadrants qppliquéd onto the palest area create enough texture to enliven the quilt. Pieced by Sue Pilarski. Appliquéd by the author, machine quilted by Joan Dawson.*

*Summer Arbor by Joan Dawson, 1993, Bothell, Washington, 55" x 55".
Joan's mastery and love of appliqué is well documented in this beautiful medallion
quilt. Fresh greens, summer pinks, and just a touch of lavender are refreshingly crisp.*

Botanical Wreath by Joan Dawson, 1993, Bothell, Washington, 64" x 79". Striking colors in an unusual combination, coupled with spectacular quilting, create a showstopper quilt. Veins of each leaf are quilted in authentic detail, giving lifelike reality to the whimsical colors.

Florida by Heki Hendrikson, 1993, Seattle, Washington, 63" x 78". Heki's sophisticated color sense is exhibited in this quilt, which combines muted greens, rusts, golds, lavenders, burgundies, and mauves. Background and border colors in half-square triangles provide a lively foundation for the wreaths' fantasy colors.

Holly Holiday *by Joan Dawson,
1993, Bothell, Washington,
29½" x 29½". The English holly
wreath is a perfect choice for a
holiday wall hanging. The bow
(provided as a creative option) and
several simple borders in holiday
prints offer a simple, yet elegant,
touch for the home.*

Christmas Laurel *by Mary Lyons
Camden, 1992, Yakima,
Washington, 28" x 28". This red-
and-green single wreath quilt adds
a lovely spot of holiday cheer. The
lattice border is a simple and
effective frame for the appliqué.
Collection of Gwen Bardes.*

Holiday Wreaths *by Mary Lyons Camden, 1993, Yakima, Washington, 52¹/₂" x 52¹/₂".*
This lovely holiday wall hanging features four red-and-green wreaths highlighted by gold
metallic embroidery. Mary chose her own two-piece swag border with leaves and tulips.

Autumn Botanica *by Laura Munson Reinstatler, 1993, Mill Creek, Washington, 73" x 88".*
Twelve wreaths, surrounded by borders of leaves, flowers, and berries, salute the beauty of nature's
work. The glorious colors of autumn set against a black background create a dramatic effect.

Chili Eucalyptus *by Joan Dawson, 1993, Bothell, Washington, 22½" x 22½". Joan thought it would be fun to appliqué the Bluegum Eucalyptus wreath in reds, creating a chili-pepper quilt just begging for a spot in the kitchen!*

Banana Eucalyptus *by Joan Dawson, 1993, Bothell, Washington, 20½" x 20½". Joan's sense of humor shows in this variation of the Bluegum Eucalyptus block. Using yellows instead of the representational blue-greens, Joan created a whimsical banana wreath that elicits smiles from all who see it.*

Bluegum Eucalyptus *by Joan Dawson, 1993, Bothell, Washington, 25" x 25". A single Bluegum Eucalyptus wreath in grayed blue-greens speaks of Joan's ties to California. The touch of lavender in the seedpods add an unexpected, but perfect, sparkle.*

Blackberry Patch *by Christine Q. Walsh, 1993, Edmonds, Washington, 16" x 16". Extensive embroidery, three-dimensional flowers, and realistic colors bring this Blackberry wreath to life. Even the stems have been embroidered with thorns! The echo-stipple hand quilting is dazzling and sets the leaves, flowers, and berries into high relief.*

Kelli's Katkins *by Jane E. Palsha, 1993, Brier, Washington, 23" x 23". Gray, burgundy, and green pussy willow sprays against a pale pink background remind us of spring's promise at winter's end. Collection of Kelli Palsha.*

Dogwood Dreams *by Nancy Lee Chong, 1993, Woodinville, Washington, 24" x 24". The flowering dogwood at the center is 80% of the pattern's original size. After appliquéing "Bonsai Wreaths," (page 39) Nancy said the 80% size seemed "so big!" She made the Log Cabin blocks into a border after using their colors for the center block's hues. Pieced by Ann Guerrero and Nancy Lee Chong. Collection of Mia Rozmyn.*

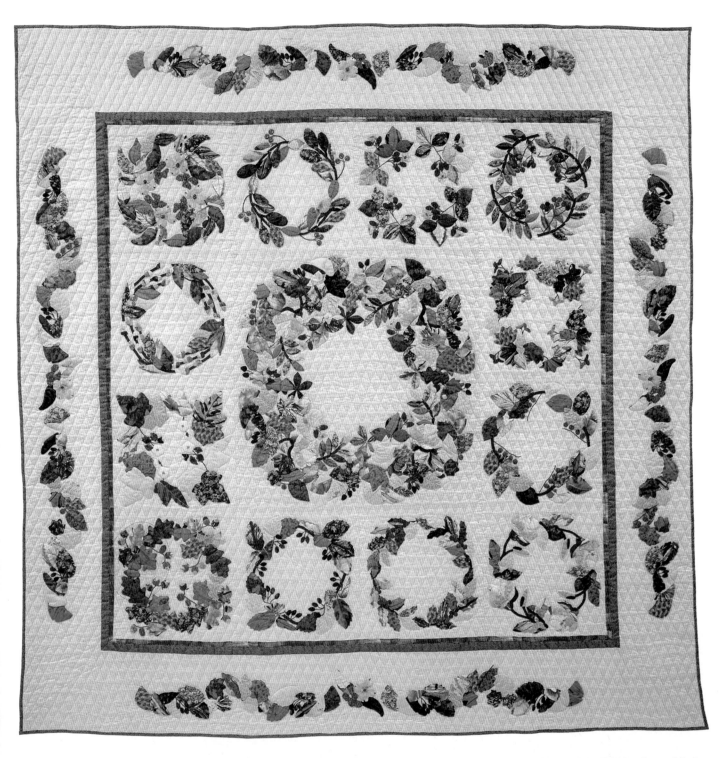

My Masterpiece *by Frieda Martinez, 1994, Everett, Washington, 92" x 92". Frieda chose fabric prints and colors to achieve a woodsy look. The twelve smaller wreaths beautifully frame the center medallion. Leaves and flowers from the 6"–8" border pattern (page 107) are appliquéd on 10"-wide borders, extending the quilt's overall dimensions.*

THE WREATH PATTERNS

THIMBLEBERRY

Rubus parviflorus

In rural areas of the Pacific Northwest, thimbleberry shrubs grow to heights of six feet. Their delicate flowers are pale cream–colored, and their bright red, raspberrylike fruit is edible but very tart and seedy. Birds and animals enjoy eating thimbleberries.

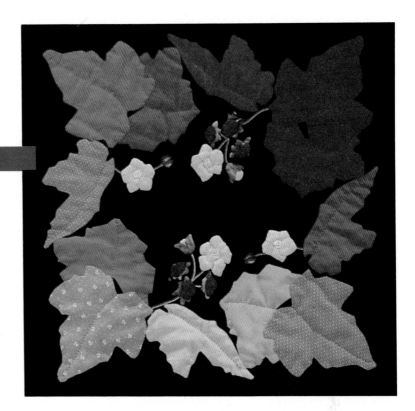

THIS BLOCK REQUIRES:

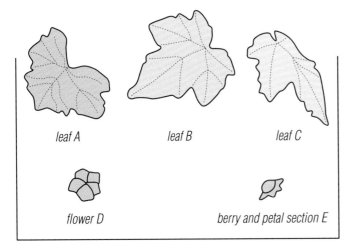

leaf A   leaf B   leaf C

flower D   berry and petal section E

4 each

berry and petal section F   bud G (2 sections)

2 each

1. Prepare the background block as described on pages 15–17.
2. Appliqué, in order, leaves A, B, and C.
3. Appliqué the flowers (D). Appliqué these flowers as single pieces of fabric, or appliqué the 5 petals individually. For a three-dimensional effect, use the option for the blackberry flowers on page 94.

   Note: Two different flower, bud, and berry motifs appear in this block. In alternate quadrants, the three-berry motif (Quadrant Plan on page 53) connects to leaf B; and the single flower/bud motif (Quadrant Plan on page 52) connects to leaf C. Refer to the photo above for placement of the motifs.

4. Appliqué each berry's (E and F) green petal section, then the red berry portion.
5. Appliqué the buds (G). First, appliqué the circular section, then the outer petals.
6. Use a stem stitch to embroider the stems and the flower petal separations (if you made flowers from one piece of fabric). Embroider the flower centers

with French knots. Embroider the tiny bud, using a stem stitch, chain stitch, or satin stitch. Embroider the leaf veins, using a stem stitch or running stitch, or quilt them later. (See pages 32–34 for embroidery stitches.)

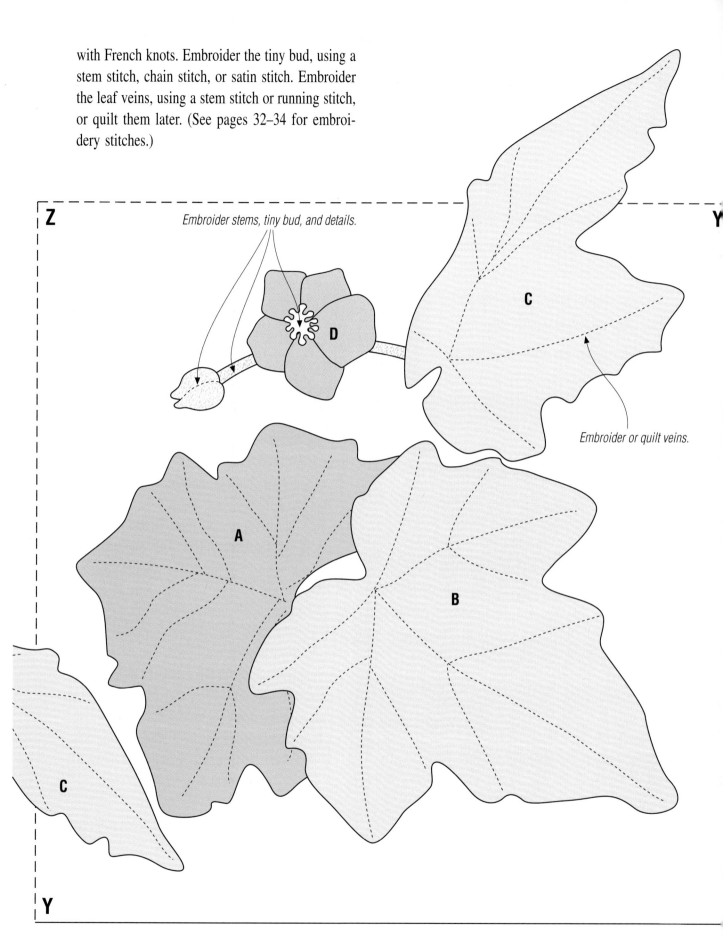

Embroider stems, tiny bud, and details.

Embroider or quilt veins.

THIMBLEBERRY QUADRANT PLAN & TEMPLATES

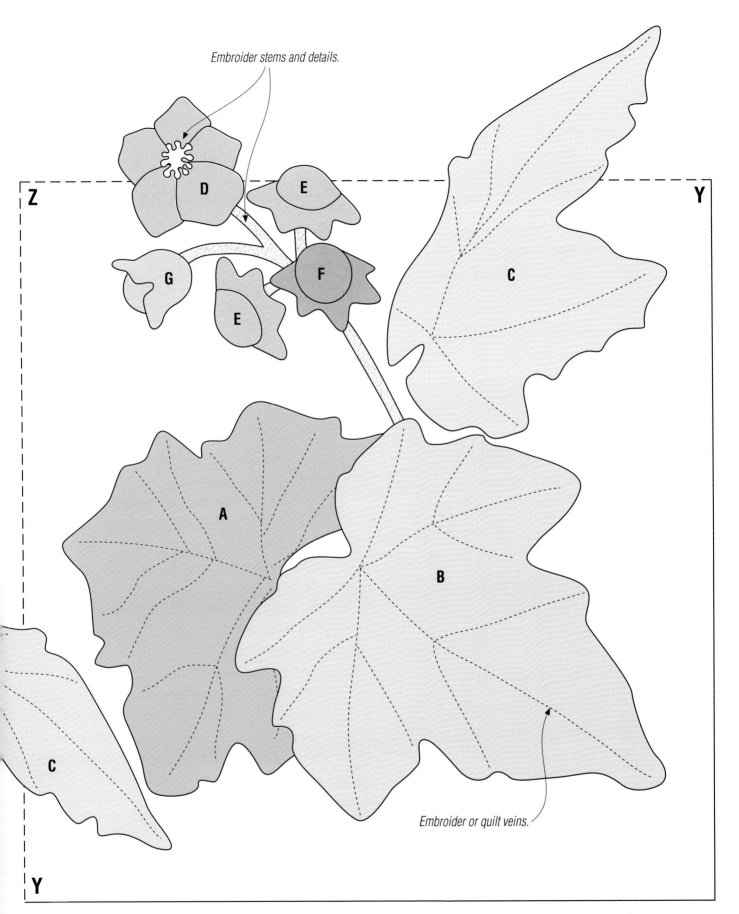

Embroider stems and details.

Z

Y

D

E

G

E

F

C

A

B

C

Y

Z

Embroider or quilt veins.

THIMBLEBERRY QUADRANT PLAN & TEMPLATES

AMERICAN (RED) MULBERRY

Morus rubra

This small to medium-sized tree is native to the Midwest and southern regions of the United States. Many songbirds, raccoons, and squirrels are attracted to its sweet and juicy berries. The berry colors range from dark red to almost black.

THIS BLOCK REQUIRES:

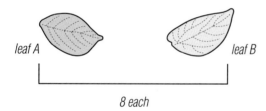

leaf A   leaf B

8 each

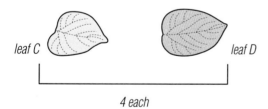

leaf C   leaf D

4 each

8 berries E

1. Prepare the background block as described on pages 15–17.
2. Appliqué each quadrant, working in a *clockwise direction* from quadrant to quadrant. Appliqué leaf A1, then leaf B1.
3. Appliqué leaves A2, then B2. Leave the tip of leaf B2 unattached in the first quadrant only. Complete the appliqué of leaf B2 when all the quadrants have been appliquéd.
4. Appliqué leaves C and D.
5. Appliqué berries E.
6. Embroider the leaf and berry stems, using a stem stitch or chain stitch. Embroider the berry details and leaf vein lines, using a stem stitch or running stitch, or quilt them later. (See pages 32–34 for embroidery stitches.)

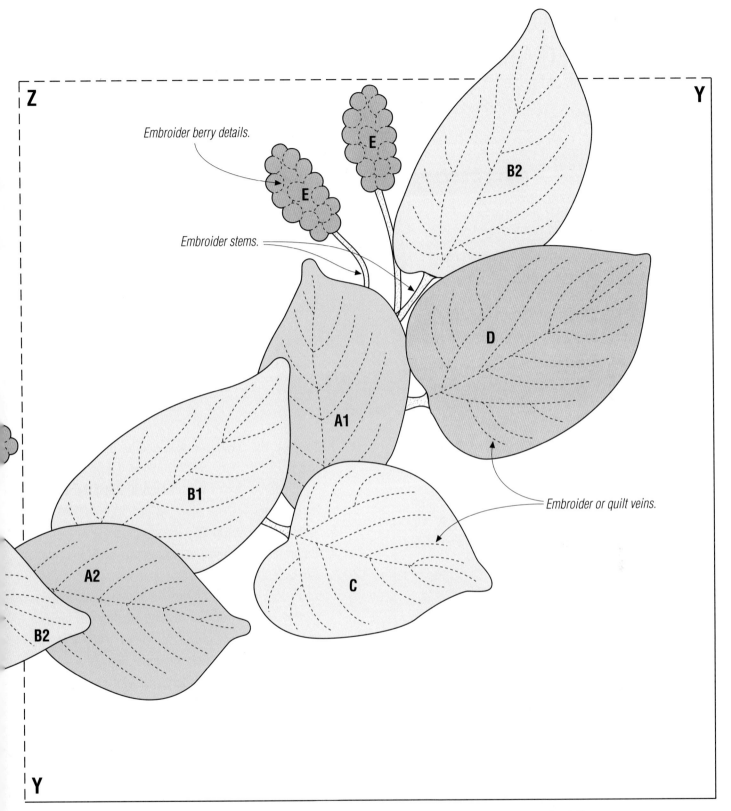

Embroider berry details.

Embroider stems.

Embroider or quilt veins.

Z

Y

Y

B2

D

A1

B1

C

A2

B2

E

E

AMERICAN (RED) MULBERRY QUADRANT PLAN & TEMPLATES

AMERICAN SYCAMORE

Platanus occidentalis

In the eastern United States, the American sycamore is one of the largest deciduous trees, often reaching heights of over one hundred feet. Its massive trunk can measure $11^1/_2$ feet in diameter! It commonly grows in lowland areas and along rivers and streams.

THIS BLOCK REQUIRES:

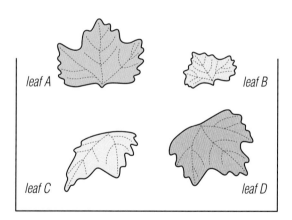

leaf A
leaf B
leaf C
leaf D

4 each

4 seedpod E

1. Prepare the background block as described on pages 15–17.
2. Appliqué the leaves in alphabetical order, quadrant by quadrant.
3. Appliqué the seedpod.
4. Embroider the stems, using a stem stitch or chain stitch. If the seedpod fabric does not resemble the seedpod's surface, embroider the texture, using closely set rows of tiny running stitches or French knots. Embroider the leaf vein lines, using a stem stitch or running stitch, or quilt them later. (See pages 32–34 for embroidery stitches.)

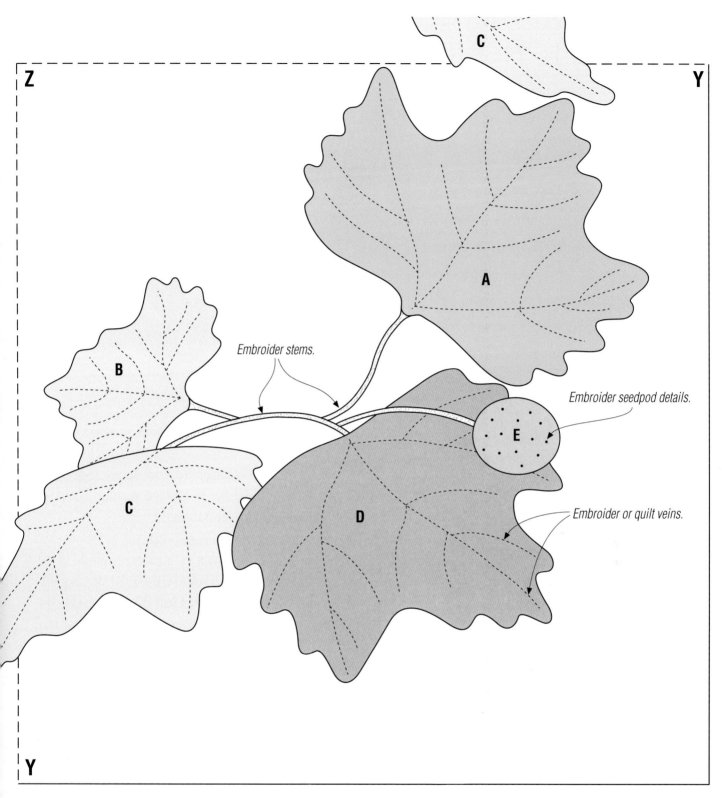

Z   Y

C

A

Embroider stems.

B

Embroider seedpod details.

E

C

D

Embroider or quilt veins.

Y

AMERICAN SYCAMORE QUADRANT PLAN & TEMPLATES

CAROLINA LAURELCHERRY

Prunus caroliniana

$\mathcal{N}$ative to the southern regions of the United States, Carolina laurelcherry is often cultivated for hedges. Its leathery evergreen leaves provide privacy year-round, and its ripened black cherries, while poisonous to humans, are eaten by birds.

THIS BLOCK REQUIRES:

4 stems, 7½" long

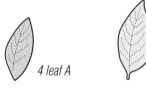

4 leaf A   *12 leaf B*

leaf C   *leaf D*

8 each

26 cherries

1. Prepare the background block as described on pages 15–17.
2. Prepare and appliqué ¼"-wide stems. (See pages 18–19.) Remember to appliqué the tiny stem segment under leaves B1 and B2.
3. Appliqué each quadrant, working in a *clockwise direction* from quadrant to quadrant. Appliqué in the following order: leaves A, C1, D1, B1, B2, B3, C2, and D2. Leave the tip of leaf B2 unattached in the first quadrant only. Complete the appliqué of leaf B2 when all the quadrants have been appliquéd.
4. Appliqué cherries and ⅛"-wide cherry stems. If you appliqué the stems, do so before the overlapping cherries are appliquéd. If you embroider the stems, appliqué all the cherries first, then embroider.
5. Add a white French knot to each cherry for a highlight. Embroider the leaf veins, using a stem stitch, or quilt them later. (See pages 32–34 for embroidery stitches.)

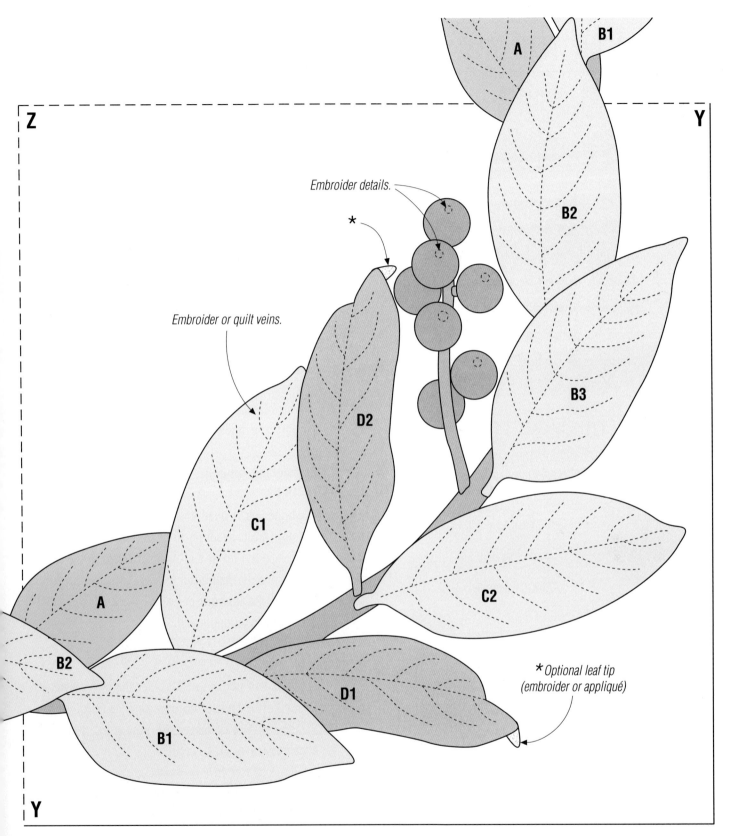

Z

Y

Embroider details.

*

Embroider or quilt veins.

B1

A

B2

B3

D2

C1

C2

A

B2

D1

*Optional leaf tip
(embroider or appliqué)

B1

Y

CAROLINA LAURELCHERRY QUADRANT PLAN & TEMPLATES

CASCARA BUCKTHORN

Rhamnus purshiana

Cascara Buckthorn is a shrub or small tree found along the west coast of North America, extending from northern California to British Columbia. Its small black berries are an important food source for birds and small mammals. In Washington and Oregon, the bark is harvested as the source of a laxative drug.

THIS BLOCK REQUIRES:

4 stems, 6" long

16 leaf A (see note)

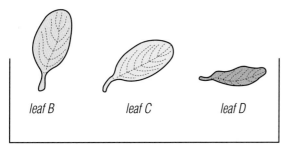

leaf B *leaf C* *leaf D*

4 each

12 berry E

Note: Leaf A4 has a different vein pattern. Otherwise, leaf A4 is identical to that of leaf A.

1. Prepare the background block as described on pages 15–17.
2. Prepare and appliqué ¹/₄"-wide stems. (See pages 18–19.)
3. Appliqué each quadrant, working in a *clockwise direction* from quadrant to quadrant. Appliqué leaf A1. Leave the tip of leaf A1 unattached in the first quadrant only. Appliqué leaves A2, A3, and A4. Complete the appliqué of leaf A1 when all the quadrants have been appliquéd.

> **OPTION**
> If you prefer to embroider the leaf stems, round off each leaf where it joins its stem.

4. Appliqué leaves B, C, and D.
5. Appliqué berries E.
6. Embroider the berry stems, using a stem stitch or chain stitch. Embroider the leaf veins, using a stem stitch or running stitch, or quilt them later. Remember to change the vein pattern in leaf A4. Embroider the berry details. (See pages 32–34 for embroidery stitches.)

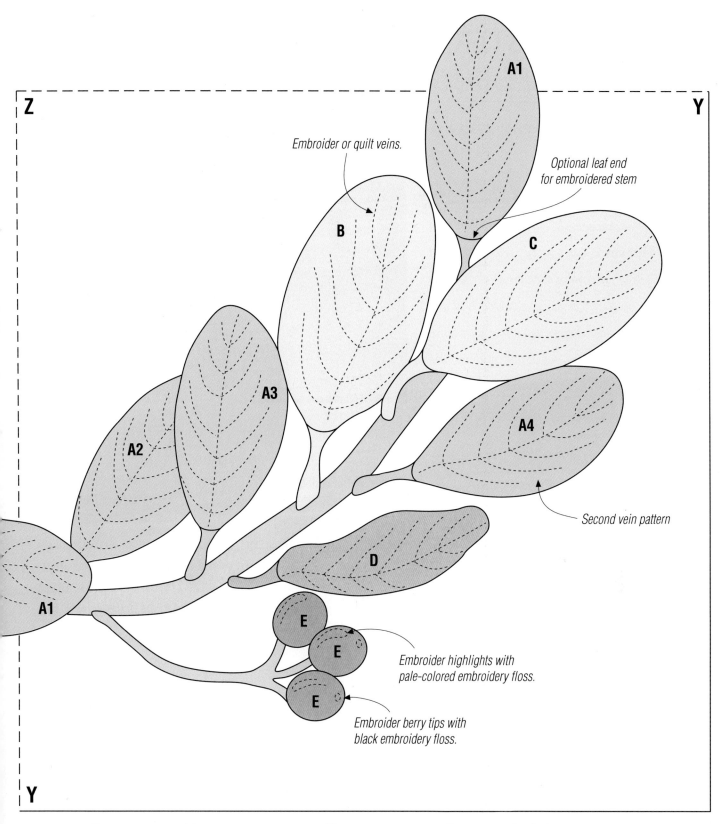

A1

Z   Y

Embroider or quilt veins.

B

Optional leaf end
for embroidered stem

C

A3

A2

A4

A1

D

Second vein pattern

E

E

Embroider highlights with
pale-colored embroidery floss.

E

Embroider berry tips with
black embroidery floss.

Y

CASCARA BUCKTHORN QUADRANT PLAN & TEMPLATES

EASTERN REDBUD
Cercis canadensis

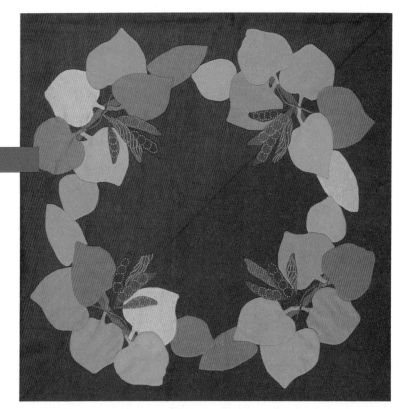

Eastern redbud and California redbud (Cercis occidentalis) are similar in appearance, although they grow in different parts of the country. Both are small trees (up to 26 feet in height) and produce showy springtime flowers that create a cloudlike profusion of pink to magenta blossoms. The reddish seedpods darken with maturity.

THIS BLOCK REQUIRES:

4 stems, 3½" long

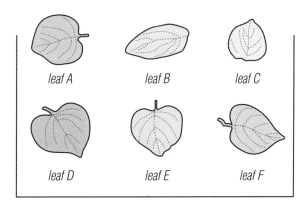

leaf A   leaf B   leaf C

leaf D   leaf E   leaf F

4 each

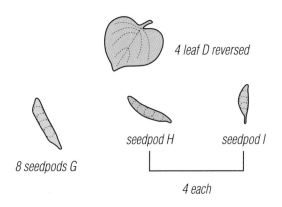

4 leaf D reversed

8 seedpods G   seedpod H   seedpod I

4 each

1. Prepare the background block as described on pages 15–17.
2. Prepare and appliqué ¼"-wide stems. (See pages 18–19.)
3. Appliqué each quadrant, working in a *clockwise direction* from quadrant to quadrant. Appliqué, in order, leaves A, B, C, D, D reversed, E, and F. Leave the tip of leaf C unattached in the first quadrant only. Complete the appliqué of leaf C when all the quadrants have been appliquéd.

> **OPTION**
>
> If you prefer to embroider the leaf stems, round off each leaf where it joins its stem.

4. Appliqué, in order, seedpods G1, G2, H, and I.
5. Embroider the leaf and seedpod stems, using a stem stitch or chain stitch. Embroider the leaf veins, using a stem stitch or running stitch, or quilt them later. Embroider the "pea" outlines in each seedpod, using a running stitch, or quilt them later. (See pages 32–34 for embroidery stitches.)

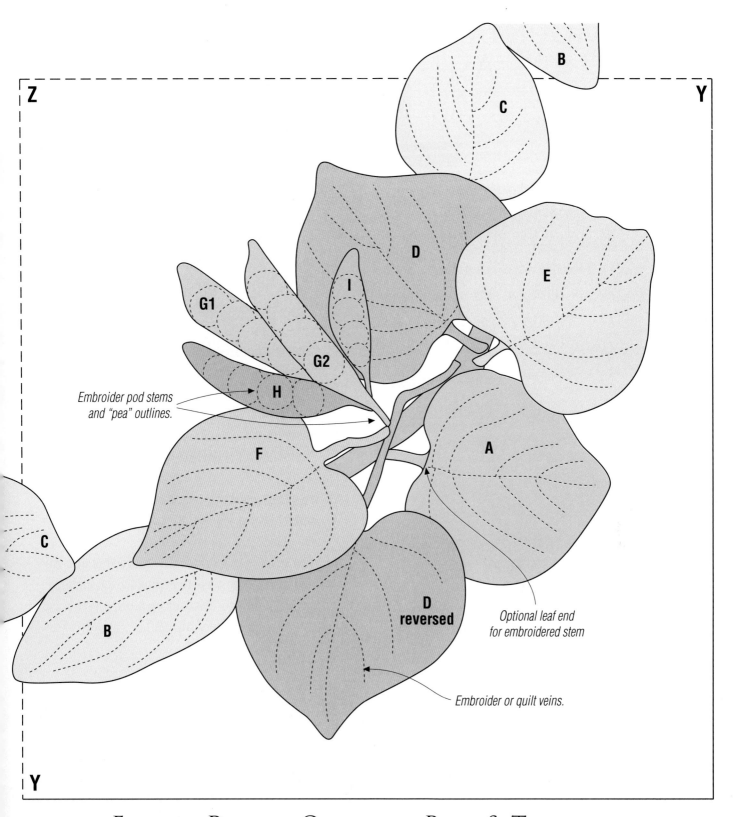

Z

Y

B

C

D

G1

I

E

G2

H

Embroider pod stems
and "pea" outlines.

F

A

D
reversed

Optional leaf end
for embroidered stem

C

B

Embroider or quilt veins.

Y

EASTERN REDBUD QUADRANT PLAN & TEMPLATES

EUROPEAN MOUNTAIN ASH

Sorbus aucuparia

*N*ative to Europe, this species of mountain ash is one of several found in the United States. They are noted for their graceful foliage and beautiful orange to bright red clusters of berries. The berries, which remain on the trees into winter, provide valuable nourishment for birds and small mammals.

THIS BLOCK REQUIRES:

4 stems, 8½" long

52 leaves

36 berries

1. Prepare the background block as described on pages 15–17.
2. Prepare and appliqué ¹/₄"- wide stems. (See pages 18–19.)
3. Appliqué the leaves, then the berries.
4. Embroider the leaf veins, using a stem stitch, or quilt them later. Embroider the berry stems, using a stem stitch or chain stitch. Use 1 strand of pale-colored embroidery floss to embroider the highlight, and black floss for the X on each berry. (See pages 32–34 for embroidery stitches.)

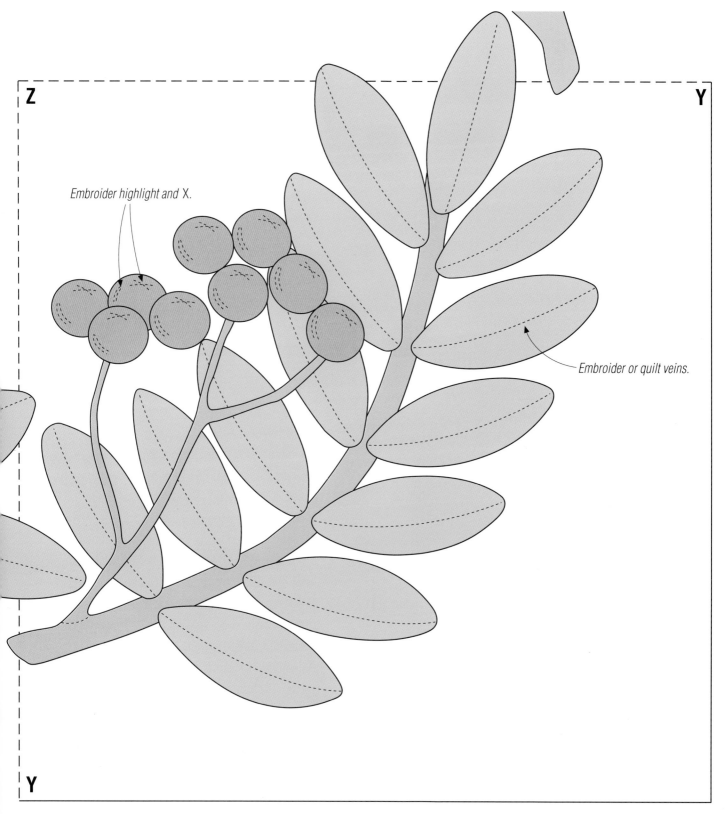

Z

Y

Embroider highlight and X.

Embroider or quilt veins.

Y

EUROPEAN MOUNTAIN ASH QUADRANT PLAN & TEMPLATES

GARRY OAK

Quercus garryana

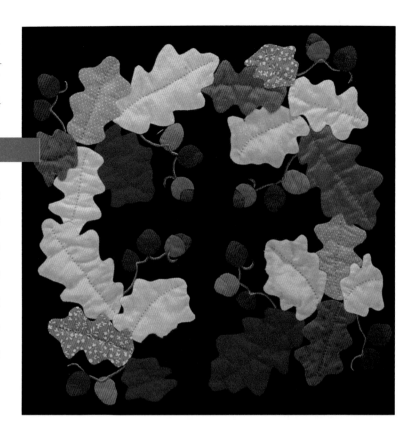

*O*aks are venerable members of the beech family and include about sixty species of trees and shrubs. Leaf and nut shapes vary widely from species to species. The leaf of the Garry oak, also called Oregon white oak, has an easily recognized and appliquéd shape. Garry oak grows along the Pacific coast, but species of oaks grow throughout North America.

THIS BLOCK REQUIRES:

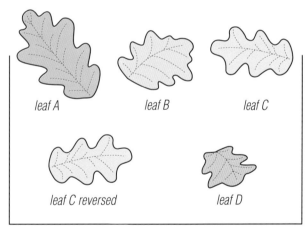

leaf A   leaf B   leaf C

leaf C reversed   leaf D

4 each

8 acorn E   12 acorn F

1. Prepare the background block as described on pages 15–17.
2. Appliqué each quadrant, working in a *counterclockwise* direction from quadrant to quadrant. Appliqué leaf A. Leave the tip of leaf A unattached in the first quadrant only. Complete the appliqué of leaf A when all the quadrants have been appliquéd.
3. Appliqué leaves B, C1, C2 reversed, and D.
4. Appliqué the upper half (part next to the stem) to the lower half of each acorn E and F. Clip the seam allowances to get a smooth curve. Finger-press the seam allowances toward the upper half, to ensure that the acorn cap fits over the lower part of the acorn. Appliqué the acorns in place on the quadrants.

Press seam allowances toward acorn cap.

5. Embroider the stems and acorn details, using a stem stitch or chain stitch. Embroider the leaf veins, using a stem stitch or running stitch, or quilt them later. (See pages 32–34 for embroidery stitches.)

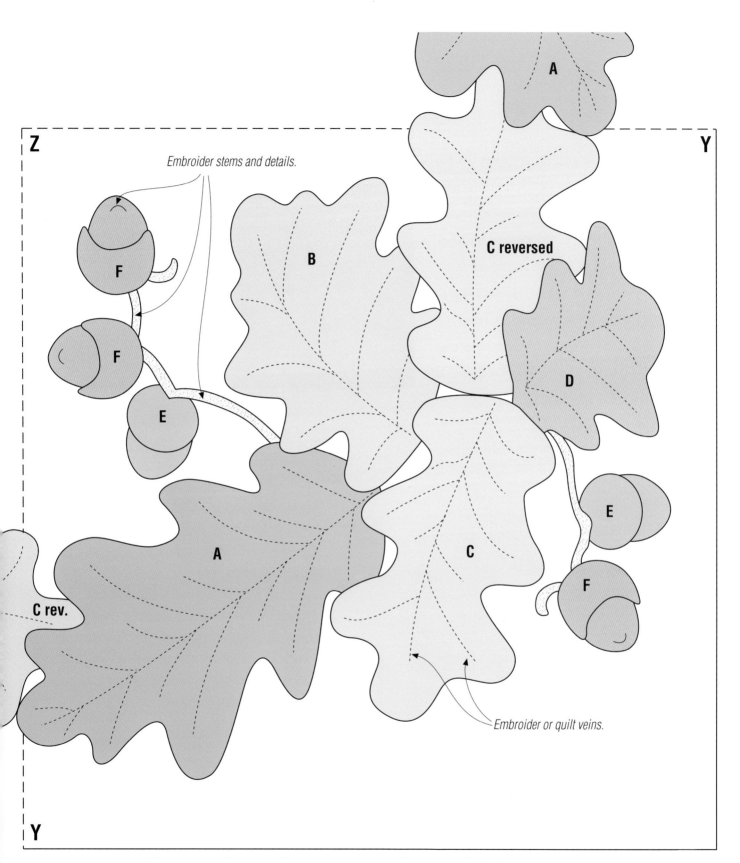

Embroider stems and details.

Z

Y

A

C reversed

F

B

F

D

E

E

A

C

C rev.

F

Embroider or quilt veins.

Y

Y

GARRY OAK QUADRANT PLAN & TEMPLATES

SALAL
Gaultheria shallon

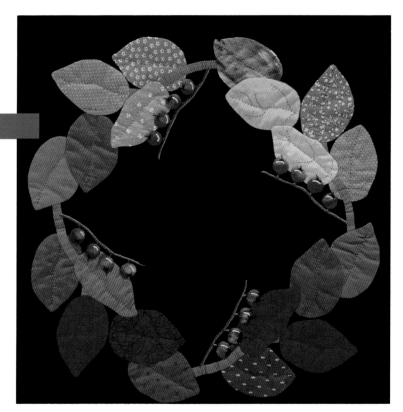

A low-growing, evergreen shrub of the Pacific Northwest, salal, with its shiny leaves, adds to the dense undergrowth of the region's forests and open areas. During childhood, in my make-believe world, the leaves were tiny pretend dinner plates or were woven into wearables! Formed from delicate waxy bell-like flowers, the berries turn red, then deep purplish black.

THIS BLOCK REQUIRES:

4 stems, 6" long

8 leaf A

leaf B   *leaf C*   *leaf D*

4 each

16 berries E

1. Prepare the background block as described on pages 15–17.
2. Appliqué each quadrant, working *clockwise* from quadrant to quadrant. Appliqué leaf C.
3. Prepare ¼"-wide stems. (See pages 18–19.) Appliqué stem across leaf C. From leaf A1 in the adjacent quadrant, curve the stem so that it will lie under leaf D as shown in the quadrant plan.
4. Appliqué leaf A1 over the stem end. Leave the tip of leaf A1 unattached in the first quadrant only. Complete the appliqué of leaf A1 when all the quadrants have been appliquéd.
5. Appliqué, in order, leaves A2, B, and D.
6. Appliqué berries E.
7. Embroider the berry stem, using a stem stitch or chain stitch. With 1 strand of black embroidery floss, embroider the berry detail, using a tiny stem stitch or a large cross-stitch. Embroider the leaf veins, using a stem stitch or running stitch, or quilt them later. (See pages 32–34 for embroidery stitches.)

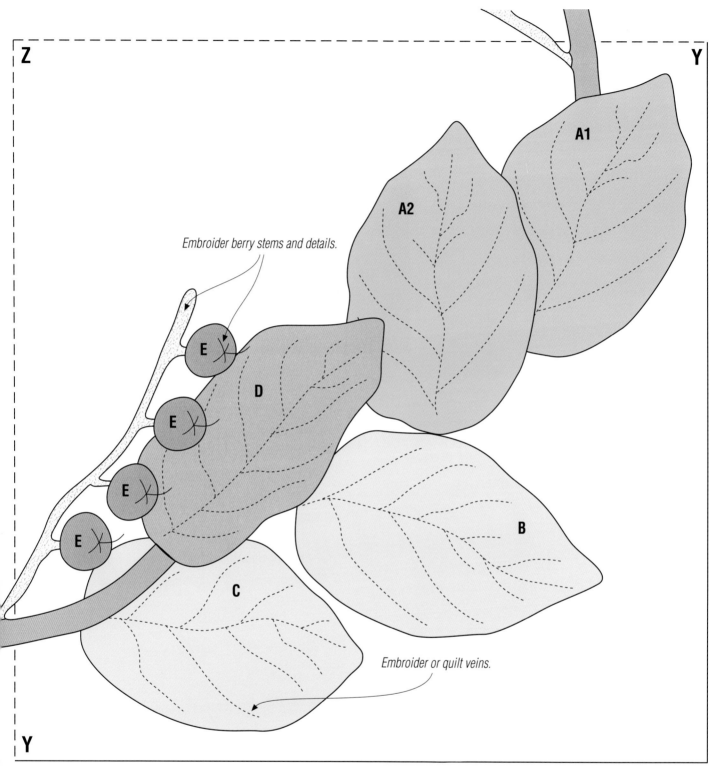

Z

Y

Embroider berry stems and details.

A2

A1

E

D

E

E

B

E

C

Embroider or quilt veins.

Y

SALAL QUADRANT PLAN & TEMPLATES

VINE MAPLE
Acer circinatum

$\mathcal{O}$ne of the true delights of a Pacific Northwest Coast autumn, the foliage of the vine maple turns scarlet. This small tree is a favorite of landscape designers, and its helicopterlike seeds provide entertainment for children as well as food for birds and small mammals.

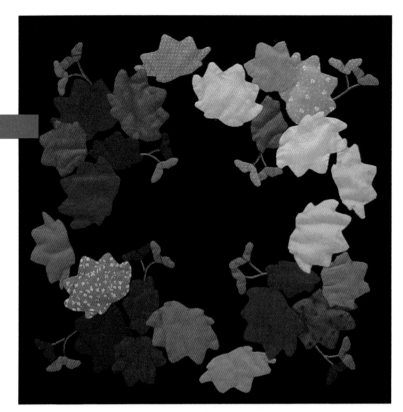

THIS BLOCK REQUIRES:

12 leaf A

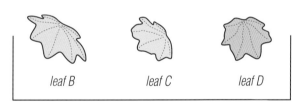

leaf B   *leaf C*   *leaf D*

4 each

Assorted scraps for 16 "helicopters"

1. Prepare the background block as described on pages 15–17.
2. Appliqué, in order, leaves A1, B, A2, C, D, and A3.
3. Appliqué the helicopters or embroider them, using a chain stitch or stem stitch. (See pages 32–34 for embroidery stitches.)
4. Embroider the stems, using a stem stitch or chain stitch, or quilt them later. Embroider the leaf veins, using a stem stitch or running stitch, or quilt them later.

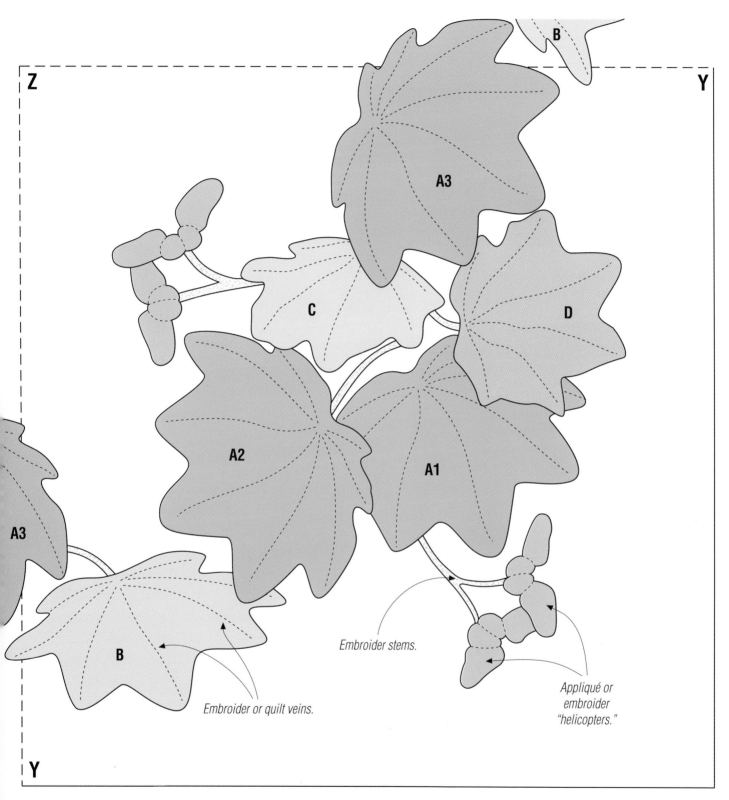

Z   Y

B

A3

C

D

A2

A1

A3

B

Embroider stems.

Embroider or quilt veins.

Appliqué or embroider "helicopters."

Y

VINE MAPLE QUADRANT PLAN & TEMPLATES

BLUEGUM EUCALYPTUS

Eucalyptus globulus

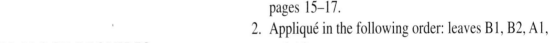

Introduced from Australia, the bluegum eucalyptus is frequently planted in California for use as a windbreak. It can reach heights of over two hundred and fifty feet. Its distinctive odor makes it easy to identify.

Note: *By changing the coloration of the leaves and omitting the berries, you can make this block into a wreath of bananas (in yellows) or chili peppers (in reds and oranges)! See the photos on page 47.*

THIS BLOCK REQUIRES:

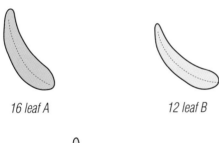

16 leaf A   *12 leaf B*

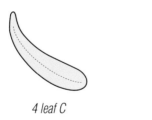

4 leaf C

8 cone D   *4 cone E*

1. Prepare the background block as described on pages 15–17.
2. Appliqué in the following order: leaves B1, B2, A1, and A2.
3. Appliqué cone D, which will be partially covered by leaf C. Choose either one fabric for the entire cone or different fabrics for the top and bottom of the cone. Appliqué the cone as one piece or two.
4. Appliqué, in order, leaves A3, A4, B3, and C.
5. Appliqué remaining cones D and E as in step 3.
6. Embroider the stems, using a stem stitch or chain stitch. Embroider the cone markings if desired, using a stem stitch or a tiny running stitch. Embroider the tiny circle in cone E, using a satin stitch. Embroider the leaf veins, using a stem stitch, or quilt them later. (See pages 32–34 for embroidery stitches.)

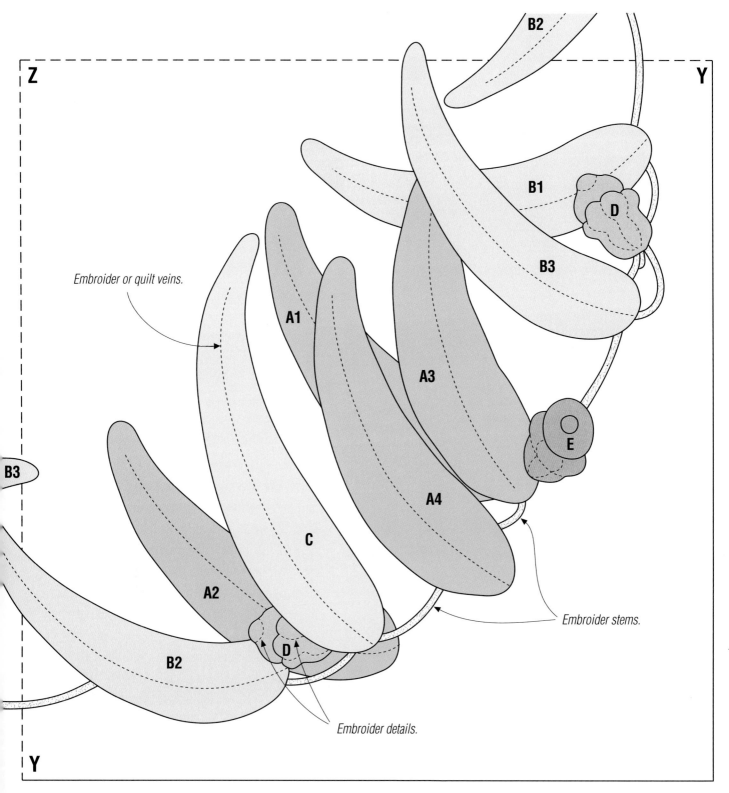

Z

Y

B2

B1

D

B3

Embroider or quilt veins.

A1

A3

E

A4

B3

C

A2

B2

D

Embroider stems.

Y

Embroider details.

BLUEGUM EUCALYPTUS QUADRANT PLAN & TEMPLATES

PUSSY WILLOW

Salix discolor

ussy willow is loved not only for its fuzzy silver catkins but for its promise that winter is nearly over. It appears in many fairy tales and has inspired nursery rhymes. Florists frequently include pussy willow in springtime bouquets.

Note: *In nature, the leaves do not appear at the same time as the fuzzy catkins as shown in the pattern.*

THIS BLOCK REQUIRES:

4 stems, 6" long
4 stems, 4½" long
4 stems, 3" long
4 stems, 2" long

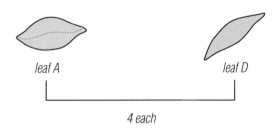

leaf A   *leaf D*

4 each

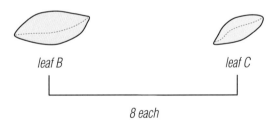

leaf B   *leaf C*

8 each

16 each of catkin and hull for pussy willow E   *12 each of catkin and hull for pussy willow F*

1. Prepare the background block as described on pages 15–17.
2. Prepare and appliqué ¼"-wide stems. (See pages 18–19.) Don't forget the short stem at the base of the leaves.
3. Appliqué leaves C1 and B1.
4. Prepare pussy willows E and F for appliqué. A quick-and-easy method is to strip-piece the catkins and hulls before cutting them out. Cut 4 or more 2" x 22" strips of dark (hull) fabrics and 3 or more 2" x 22" strips of light (catkin) fabrics. Sew them into strip-pieced units, alternating dark and light strips as shown. Use different darks and lights for a more varied look or use only one dark and one light for a more traditional look.

   Press seam allowances toward the dark strips. Use the catkin/hull template (adding ¼"-wide seam allowances) to cut the pieces from the strip-pieced unit as shown. To get different dark/light combinations, move the template around the strip-pieced unit. Prepare the pieces for appliqué.

   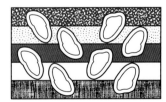

5. Appliqué all catkins except the pussy willow E that overlaps leaf A.

6. Appliqué in the following order: leaves D, B2, C2, and A.

7. Appliqué pussy willow E so that it overlaps leaf A.

8. Embroider the leaf veins, using a stem stitch or running stitch, or quilt them later. (See pages 32–34 for embroidery stitches.)

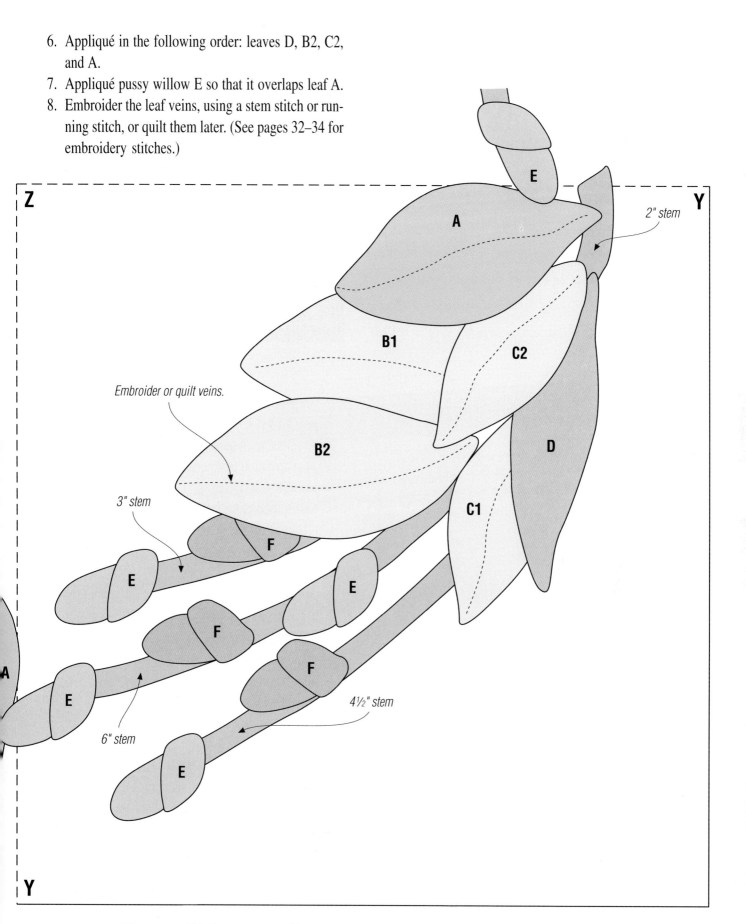

PUSSY WILLOW QUADRANT PLAN & TEMPLATES

FLOWERING DOGWOOD

Cornus florida

$\mathcal{T}$he flowering dogwood is cherished for its showy white to pink blossoms that appear before the tree leafs out in the spring. It grows in the eastern half of the United States and is a favorite among quilters for its design inspirations. The Pacific dogwood (Cornus nuttallii), found along the Pacific coast, is similar, except its petals have no notches.

THIS BLOCK REQUIRES:

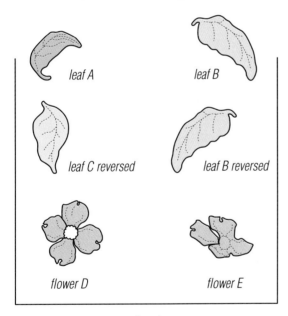

leaf A

leaf B

leaf C reversed

leaf B reversed

flower D

flower E

4 each

12 leaf C

flower centers

Note: Cut each flower in one piece, or cut four separate petals. Cut a center for each flower.

1. Prepare the background block as described on pages 15–17.
2. Appliqué each quadrant, working in a *counterclockwise direction* from quadrant to quadrant. Appliqué leaf C1. Leave the tip of leaf C1 unattached in the first quadrant only. Complete the appliqué of leaf C1 when all the quadrants have been appliquéd.
3. Appliqué leaves A, B, C2, C3, and C reversed.
4. Appliqué leaf B reversed.
5. Appliqué the flowers D and E, overlapping the petals as you go. If you appliqué the flowers as whole pieces, clip the petals carefully to separate them because the seam allowances are tiny.

   Clip
   Clip
   Clip
   Clip

6. Appliqué the flower centers.
7. Embroider the contour lines on the flower petals, using a stem stitch. Embroider 4 satin stitches as shown to define the petals' outer notches. Add several French knots to the flower centers for texture. Embroider leaf veins, using a stem stitch, or quilt them later. (See pages 32–34 for embroidery stitches.)

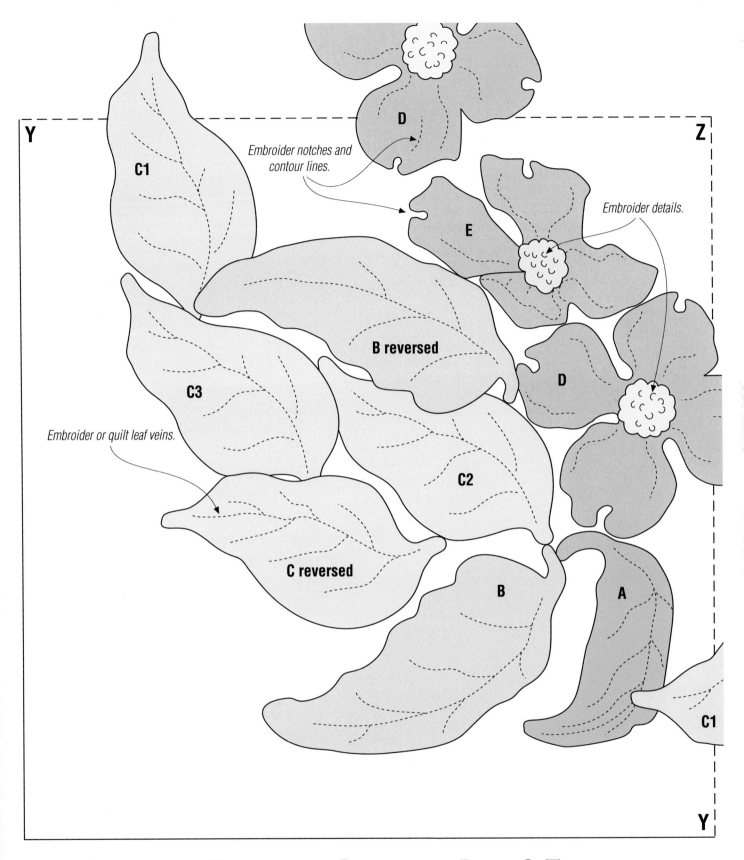

Y

Z

C1

Embroider notches and contour lines.

D

E

Embroider details.

D

B reversed

C3

Embroider or quilt leaf veins.

C2

C reversed

B

A

C1

Y

FLOWERING DOGWOOD QUADRANT PLAN & TEMPLATES

GINKGO

Ginkgo biloba

*T*his ancient species is native to southeastern China and is the only surviving genus in its family. Ginkgo leaves today remain largely unchanged from the fossils of its leaves eons ago. Ginkgos are planted as ornamentals in North America, can attain heights of 65 to 100 feet, and can withstand poor soil conditions and polluted air.

THIS BLOCK REQUIRES:

4 stems, 8" long

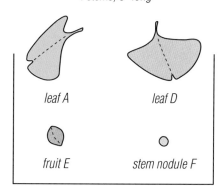

leaf A   leaf D

fruit E   stem nodule F

8 each

leaf C leaf C reversed stem nodule G

4 each

12 leaf B

1. Prepare the background block as described on pages 15–17.
2. Prepare and appliqué ¼"-wide stems. (See pages 18–19.)
3. Appliqué the stem nodules to which the leaves are attached. The nodules should be the same color as the stems.
4. Appliqué each quadrant, working in a *counterclockwise direction* from quadrant to quadrant. Appliqué, in order, leaves A1, B1, B2, and D1. Leave the tip of leaf B1 unattached in the first quadrant only. Complete the appliqué of leaf B1 when all the quadrants have been appliquéd.

OPTION

If you prefer to embroider the leaf stems, round off each leaf where it joins its stem.

---

5. Appliqué leaves A2, B3, C reversed, C1, and D2.
6. Appliqué the fruits E.
7. Embroider the leaf stems, using a stem stitch or chain stitch. Embroider the lines on each fruit, using a stem stitch. Embroider the leaf veins, using a stem stitch, or quilt them later. (See pages 32–34 for embroidery stitches.)

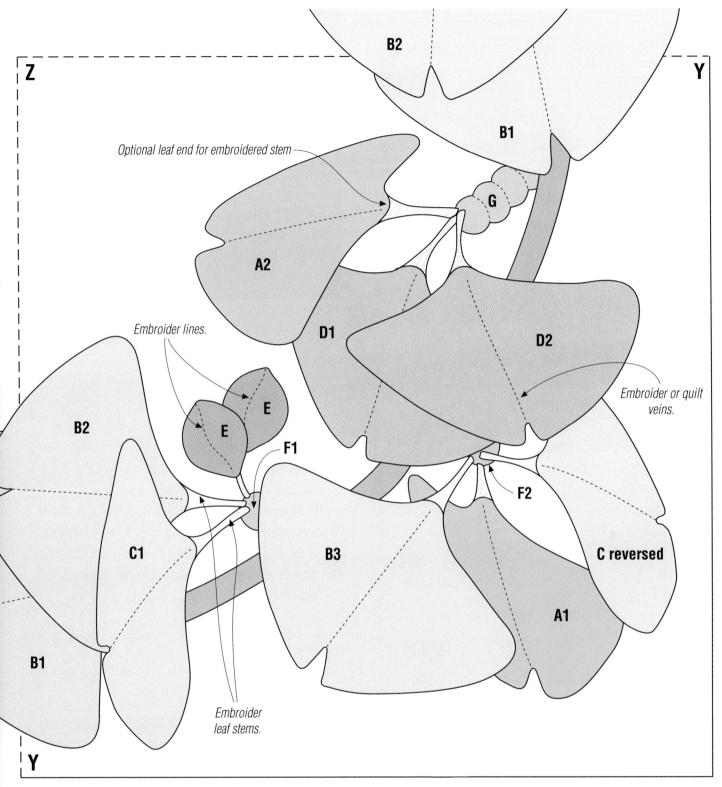

Z

Y

B2

B1

Optional leaf end for embroidered stem

G

A2

D1

D2

Embroider or quilt veins.

Embroider lines.

E

E

B2

F1

F2

C1

B3

C reversed

B1

A1

Embroider leaf stems.

Y

GINKGO QUADRANT PLAN & TEMPLATES

HORSECHESTNUT

Aesculus hippocastanum

*H*orsechestnut trees, introduced to North America during colonial times, are often planted along streets or in parks. Their majestic shape and size provides cool shade during the summer. The spiny yellow-green seedpods split open to reveal a smooth coffee-colored buckeye inside.

THIS BLOCK REQUIRES:

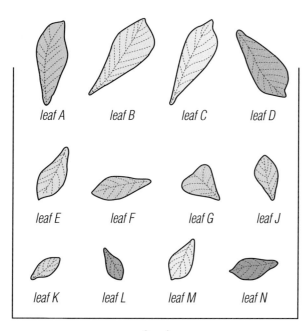

leaf A leaf B leaf C leaf D

leaf E leaf F leaf G leaf J

leaf K leaf L leaf M leaf N

8 each

8 seedpods H
8 buckeyes I

1. Prepare the background block as described on pages 15–17.
2. Appliqué, in order, large leaves A, B, C, D, E, F, and G in all 4 quadrants.
3. To make each horsechestnut, cut 1 seedpod H and 1 buckeye I. The seedpod circle has a ¼"-wide seam allowance, and the buckeye does not. Place the seedpod circle over the buckeye circle and pin or baste to the background block. Appliqué around the seedpod circle. Carefully cut only the seedpod circle along the dotted line. Turn these edges under and use reverse appliqué (pages 25–26) to reveal the buckeye underneath.

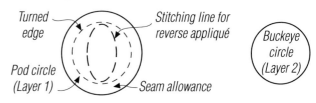

Turned edge
Stitching line for reverse appliqué
Pod circle (Layer 1)
Seam allowance
Buckeye circle (Layer 2)

4. Appliqué all small leaves J, K, L, M, and N.
5. Embroider the leaf and horsechestnut stems, using a stem stitch or chain stitch. Outline the area on the horsechestnuts where the seedpod meets the buckeye, using a tiny buttonhole stitch. Embroider the spiny points on the seedpods, using 2 short, single stitches. Embroider the leaf veins, using a stem stitch, or quilt them later. (See pages 32–34 for embroidery stitches.)

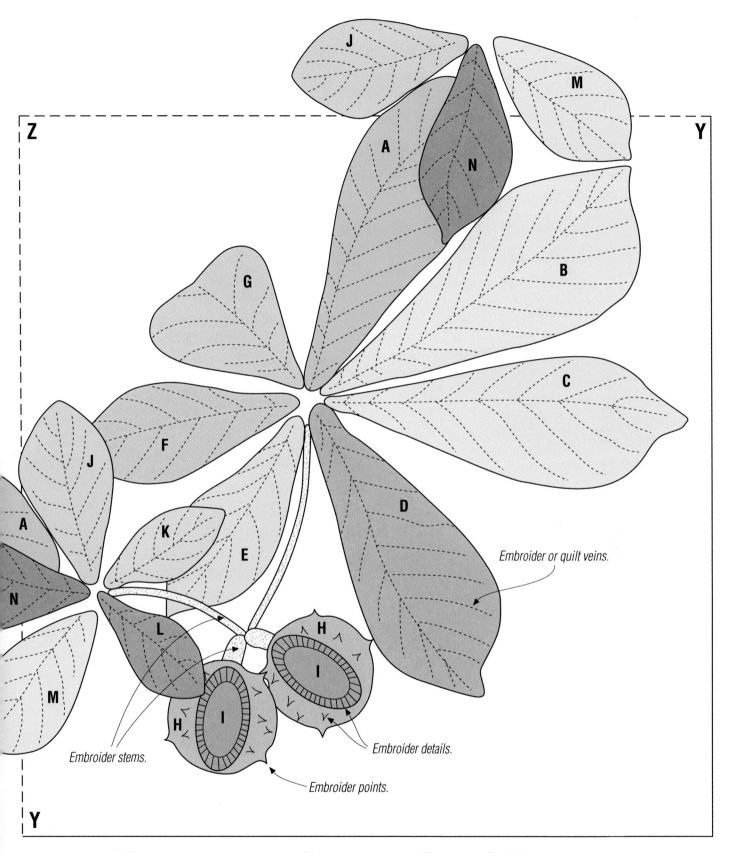

Embroider or quilt veins.

Embroider details.

Embroider stems.

Embroider points.

HORSECHESTNUT QUADRANT PLAN & TEMPLATES

MAGNOLIA

Magnolia soulangeana

*S*howy white and pink-to-purple magnolias bloom in early spring before they "leaf out." The entire shrub is covered with 5"–10" blossoms, creating a dramatic display. Also called saucer magnolia or Chinese magnolia, it is widely planted throughout the United States.

Note: *In nature, the flowers appear before foliage growth, not at the same time as shown in the pattern.*

THIS BLOCK REQUIRES:

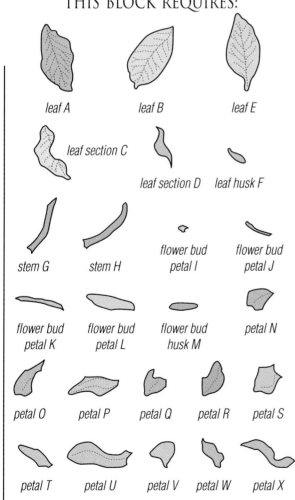

leaf A   leaf B   leaf E

leaf section C

leaf section D   leaf husk F

stem G   stem H   flower bud petal I   flower bud petal J

flower bud petal K   flower bud petal L   flower bud husk M   petal N

petal O   petal P   petal Q   petal R   petal S

petal T   petal U   petal V   petal W   petal X

4 each

1. Prepare the background block as described on pages 15–17.
2. Appliqué each quadrant, working in a *counterclockwise* direction from quadrant to quadrant. Appliqué leaf A.
3. Prepare and appliqué stem G, then stem H.
4. Appliqué leaf B, then E. Appliqué leaf section C, then leaf section D. Appliqué leaf husk F, using a different value of the stem color.
5. Appliqué the flower bud, beginning with tip I and continuing in alphabetical order through L.
6. Appliqué flower bud husk M. Husk M and the embroidered tiny husk next to it are of a color similar to the stems.
7. Appliqué the flower, beginning with petal N and continuing in alphabetical order through petal X. Leave the tip of petal U unattached in the first quadrant only. Complete the appliqué of petal U when all the quadrants have been appliquéd.
8. Embroider the tiny husk on the bud, using a stem stitch, satin stitch, or chain stitch. Embroider the veins on the leaves, using a stem stitch or running stitch, or quilt them later. Embroider the contour lines on the flower petals, using a stem stitch. (See pages 32–34 for embroidery stitches.)

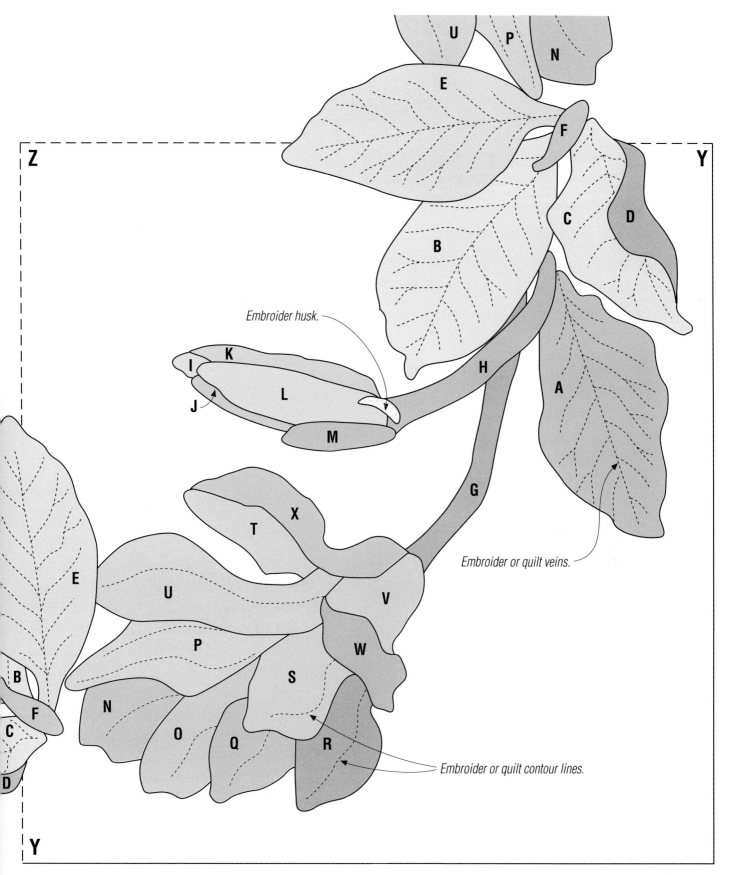

Embroider husk.

Embroider or quilt veins.

Embroider or quilt contour lines.

MAGNOLIA QUADRANT PLAN & TEMPLATES

TULIP TREE

Liriodendron tulipifera

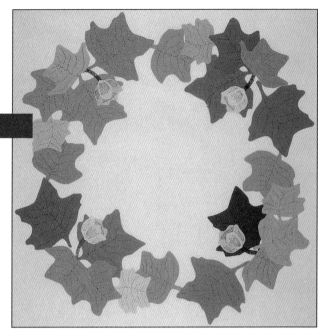

The tulip tree (also known as yellow poplar) reaches from the east coast to the midwestern section of the United States. A member of the magnolia family, this tree grows in deciduous forests and ornamental gardens. The flowers measure 1½"–2" in diameter and are green with an orange-colored base. The fruits and seeds provide a food source for birds, rabbits, squirrels, and mice.

THIS BLOCK REQUIRES:

4 stems, ⅛" wide, 1½" long*

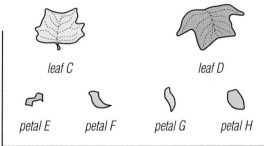

leaf A   leaf B

8 each

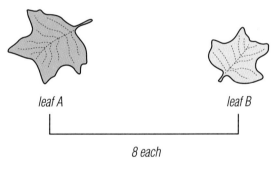

leaf C   leaf D

petal E   petal F   petal G   petal H

4 each

*If you prefer, embroider each tulip flower's stem after appliqué in the block is complete.

 Wreath Patterns

1. Prepare the background block as described on pages 15–17.
2. Appliqué leaf A1, then leaf B1, which overlaps the quadrant line.

> **OPTION**
> If you prefer to embroider the leaf stems, round off each leaf where it joins its stem.

3. Appliqué in the following order: leaves C, B2, and A2.
4. Prepare ⅛"-wide "tulip" stem for appliqué. (See pages 18–19.) If you prefer, embroider the stem when all appliqué is complete.
5. Appliqué, in order, flower petals E, F, G, and H.
6. Appliqué leaf D.
7. Embroider the details on flower petal E, using a tiny buttonhole stitch. Embroider the lines on petals F, G, and H, using a tiny stem stitch or long single stitches. Use 3 or 4 rows of stem stitches or chain stitches to embroider the flower stem if you haven't appliquéd it. Embroider the leaf stems, using a stem stitch or chain stitch. Embroider the leaf veins, using a stem stitch or running stitch, or quilt them later. (See pages 32–34 for embroidery stitches.)

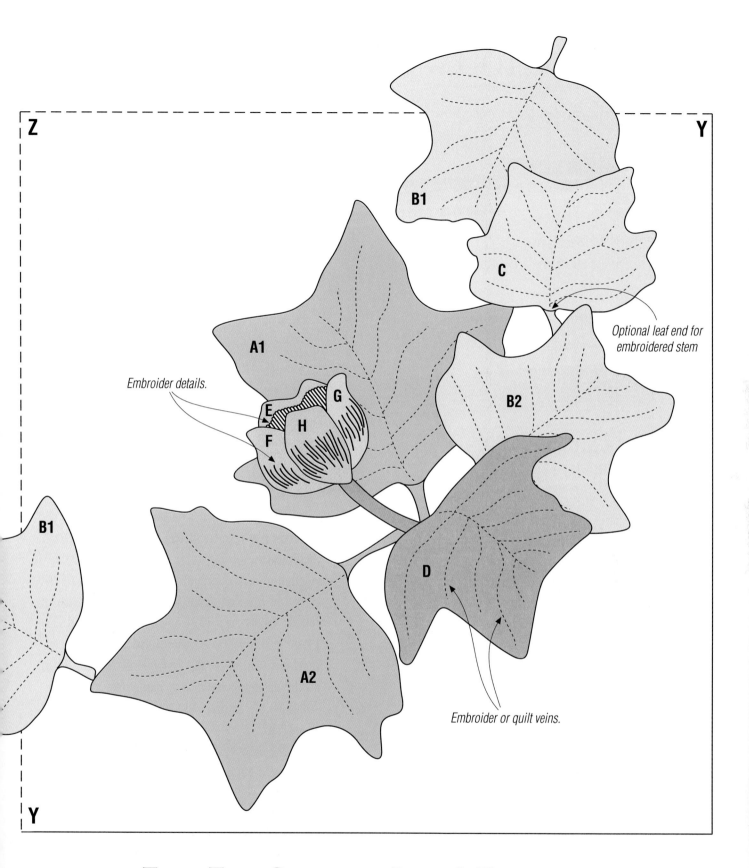

Z Y

Embroider details.

B1

C

Optional leaf end for
embroidered stem

A1

E G
H
F

B2

B1

D

Embroider or quilt veins.

A2

Y

TULIP TREE QUADRANT PLAN & TEMPLATES

ENGLISH HOLLY

Ilex aquifolium

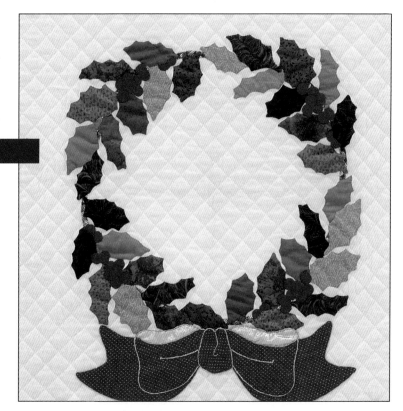

Of the many species of holly, the English holly is the best known. It was brought to the colonies from England. Its shiny, dense leaves and bright red berries are a part of many traditional Christmas wreaths, swags, and floral arrangements. A single English holly wreath block makes a lovely wall hanging or small quilt. Appliqué the optional bow or add a border to enhance your holiday decor.

THIS BLOCK REQUIRES:

4 stems, 8¼" long

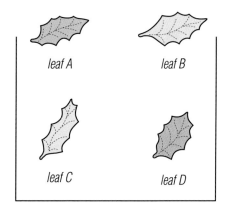

leaf A   leaf B

leaf C   leaf D

8 each

4 leaf E

40 berries

1. Prepare the background block as described on pages 15–17.
2. Prepare ¹/₄"-wide stems. (See pages 18–19.) Appliqué stems. Each 8¼" stem curves around the quadrant from the tip of leaf A1 (from the adjacent quadrant).
3. Appliqué each quadrant, working in a *clockwise* direction from quadrant to quadrant. Appliqué, in order, leaves A1, B1, C1, B2, C2, D1, and D2. Leave the tip of leaf A1 unattached in the first quadrant only. Complete the appliqué of leaf A1 when all the quadrants have been appliquéd.
4. Appliqué the 2 berries that will be partially covered by leaf A2.
5. Appliqué leaves A2 and E.
6. Appliqué the large cluster of berries.
7. Embroider a white or light-colored French knot on each berry (in approximately the same location) for highlights. Embroider the leaf veins, using a stem stitch or running stitch, or quilt them later. (See pages 32–34 for embroidery stitches.)

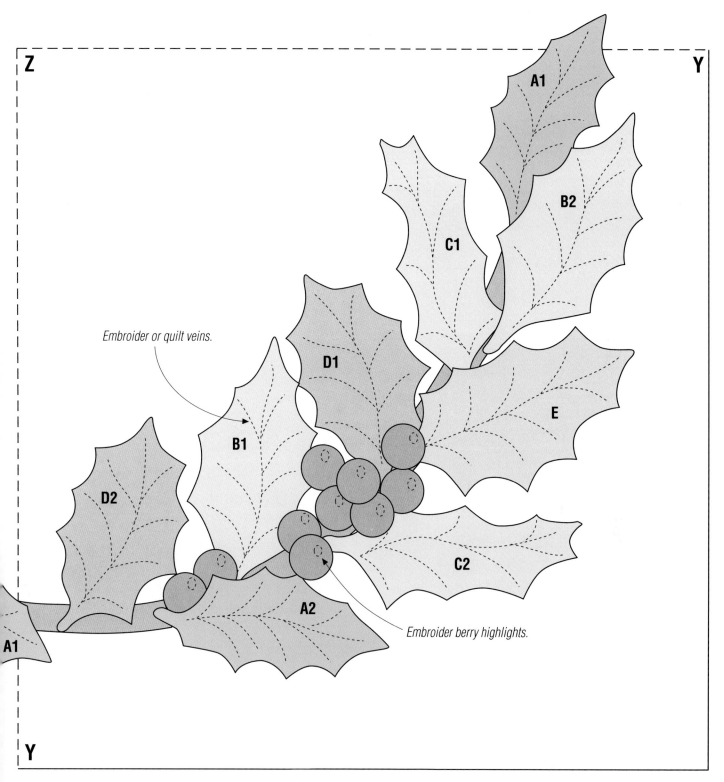

Z   Y

A1

B2

C1

Embroider or quilt veins.

D1

B1

E

D2

A2

C2

Embroider berry highlights.

A1

Y

ENGLISH HOLLY QUADRANT PLAN & TEMPLATES

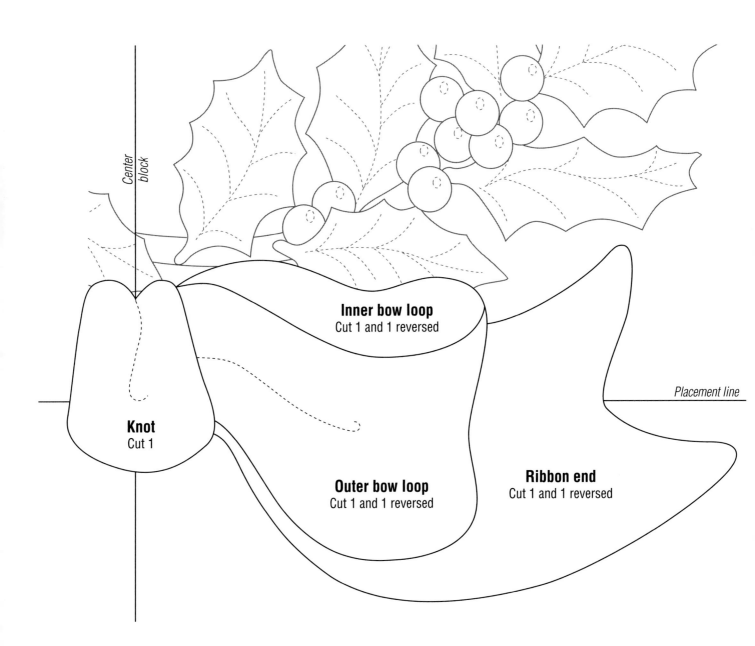

Center block

Placement line

Inner bow loop
Cut 1 and 1 reversed

Knot
Cut 1

Outer bow loop
Cut 1 and 1 reversed

Ribbon end
Cut 1 and 1 reversed

HOLIDAY BOW TEMPLATE

Special Holiday Wreath

A big ribbon bow at the bottom of an English holly wreath spills onto a 2¹/₂" border. Add more borders if you prefer.

1. Appliqué the English holly wreath according to the directions.
2. Add a 2¹/₂" border (or combination of borders).
3. Appliqué the 2 ribbon ends on the wreath, referring to the placement line on the templates.
4. Appliqué each outer bow loop to its inner bow loop. Clip as necessary to get smooth curves. Treating the joined inner and outer

bow loops as one piece, paper-piece them, then appliqué to the wreath.

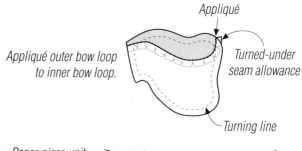

Appliqué

Appliqué outer bow loop to inner bow loop.

Turned-under seam allowance

Turning line

Paper-piece unit first, then appliqué 2-piece unit to background block.

Paper

5. Appliqué the knot in place.
6. Add more borders if you prefer, then quilt and bind. Remember to label your quilt!

RED ALDER

Alnus rubra

*R*ed alder grows prolifically in the Pacific Northwest from southern Alaska to northern California. When mature, it reaches as tall as 132 feet. Its fast growth provides protection for the slower-maturing evergreen species during their early years. Red alder is used in smoking meats, and its tiny cones are often used as castings for jewelry.

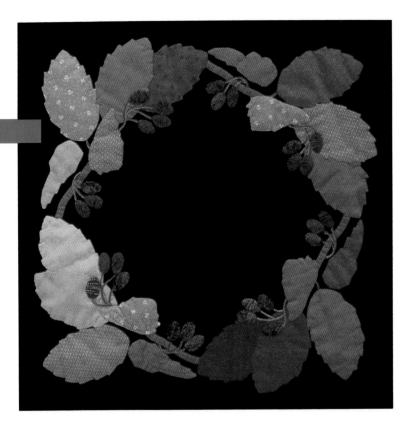

THIS BLOCK REQUIRES:

4 stems, 3½" long

12 leaf A

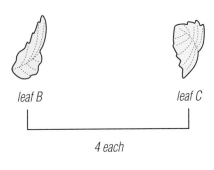

leaf B   *leaf C*

4 each

28 alder cone D*

*If you prefer, embroider the alder cones.

1. Prepare the background block as described on pages 15–17.
2. Prepare and appliqué ¼"-wide stems. (See pages 18–19.)
3. Appliqué each quadrant, working in a *counterclockwise direction* from quadrant to quadrant. Appliqué, in order, leaves A1, A2, and A3. Leave the tip of leaf A1 unattached in the first quadrant only. Complete the appliqué of leaf A1 when all the quadrants have been appliquéd.
4. Appliqué leaves B and C.
5. Appliqué cones D or embroider them, using a random line of buttonhole stitches, chain stitches, or French knots. (See pages 32–34 for embroidery stitches.) For a three-dimensional cone effect, refer to the option on page 92.
6. Embroider the cone stems, using a stem or chain stitch. Embroider the leaf veins, using a stem or running stitch, or quilt them later.

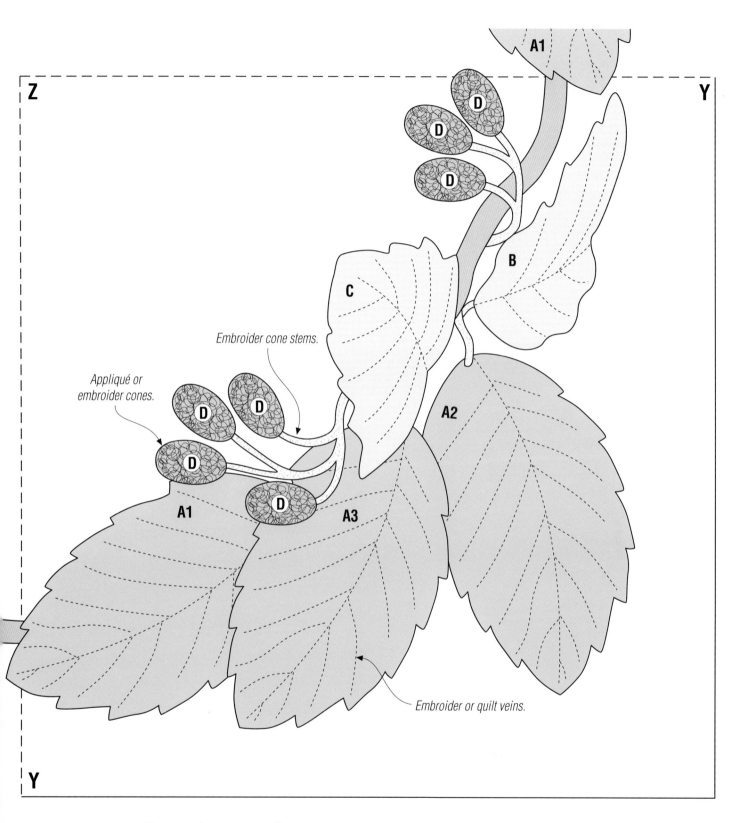

Z

Y

A1

D
D
D

D

C

B

Embroider cone stems.

Appliqué or
embroider cones.

D
D

D

A2

D

A1

A3

Embroider or quilt veins.

Y

RED ALDER QUADRANT PLAN & TEMPLATES

Three-Dimensional Alder Cones

1. Cut 4 bias strips of fabric, each $1^{3}/_{8}$" x 18". Cut the strips into 28 pieces, each $2^{1}/_{2}$" long.

2. With right sides together, fold each piece in half lengthwise. Hand stitch across one end and along the length of the segment, using $^{1}/_{8}$"-long running stitches as shown. Do not tie a knot when you are finished basting. Leave the needle threaded.

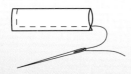

3. Trim the seam allowances to $^{1}/_{8}$".

4. Turn the tube right side out.

5. Gently pull the thread, gathering the tube of fabric as tightly as possible. Make two tiny stitches to secure the gathering.

6. Turn the raw edges under and stitch the end of the tube closed.

7. Place the gathered edge of the alder cone on the background block. Pin or baste in place. Arrange the gathers, then pin or baste the folds of the ungathered side to secure them.

8. Appliqué the cone in place.

BLACKBERRY

Rubus procerus

ℋimalayan blackberry plants, which can reach heights of 10 feet, grow prolifically in the Pacific Northwest. They are considered a pest by gardeners because of their persistent growth and thorny stalks. The succulent and flavorful berries are a favorite for pies, cobblers, and preserves.

Note: *Himalayan blackberry plants actually have five leaflets instead of the three pictured in the pattern.*

THIS BLOCK REQUIRES:

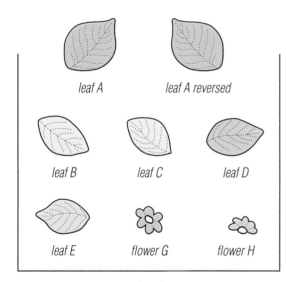

leaf A   leaf A reversed

leaf B   leaf C   leaf D

leaf E   flower G   flower H

4 each

48 small scraps of fabric for berry "petals"   24 berries F

1. Prepare the background block as described on pages 15–17.
2. Appliqué ¹/₈"-wide stems. (See pages 18–19.) If you prefer, embroider the stems, using a stem stitch or chain stitch, before you appliqué the leaves, or wait until you have finished the appliqué.
3. Appliqué leaves A and A reversed, then leaves B, C, D, and E.
4. Appliqué flowers G and H or embroider the flowers, using a chain stitch or satin stitch. (See pages 32–34.) For a three-dimensional effect, see the instructions below.
5. Prepare each berry for appliqué, then appliqué around only the lower part of the berry; leave the upper part open for the berry "petals."
6. Make berry "petals" by folding a ⁷/₈"-diameter circle or a ⁷/₈" x ⁷/₈" square of petal fabric in half, wrong sides together. Fold again into thirds as shown. Make 2 petals for each berry.

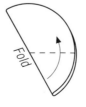

Fold

Fold   *Trim if necessary.*

7. Tuck 2 petals under the top of each berry as shown. Pin in place. Appliqué petals, then the rest of the blackberry.

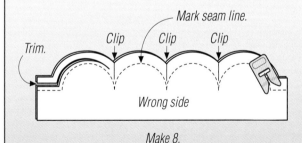

8. Use French knots to embroider the flower centers. Embroider the stems, using a stem stitch or chain stitch. Embroider the leaf veins, using a stem stitch or running stitch, or quilt them later. (See pages 32–34 for embroidery stitches.)

 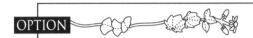

Three-Dimensional Blackberry Flowers

This technique creates a larger, more stylized flower with a fewer than botanically accurate number of petals. It makes a three-dimensional focal point for the block. You can use this technique for the Thimbleberry flower too (page 51). Make 8.

1. For each flower, cut out 2 fabric pieces, using the Three-Dimensional Flower templates on page 95. Choose either the same fabric or two different values for a shaded effect.

2. With right sides together, use a short stitch (16 stitches per inch) to carefully hand or machine stitch along the scalloped edge. Trim seam allowances to ⅛" and carefully clip into each notch. Be careful not to cut through the stitching.

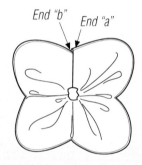

Mark seam line.

Trim.

Clip   Clip   Clip

Wrong side

Make 8.

3. Turn right side out and press.

4. Machine or hand baste along the straight raw edges and gather tightly.

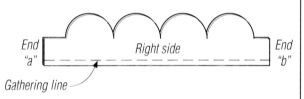

End "a"   *Right side*   End "b"

Gathering line

5. Fold the longer end "a" over the short end "b" and stitch to secure.

End "b"   End "a"

6. Adjust the gathers if necessary and baste in place on the background block.

7. Prepare the flower center and appliqué in place.

8. Embroider the flower center with French knots for added texture. (See page 34.)

Wreath Patterns

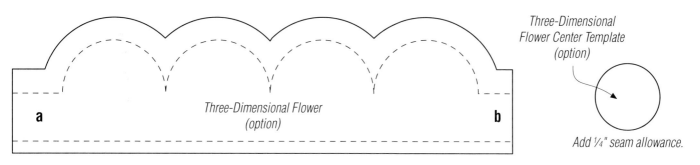

Three-Dimensional Flower (option)

a

b

Three-Dimensional Flower Center Template (option)

Add ¼" seam allowance.

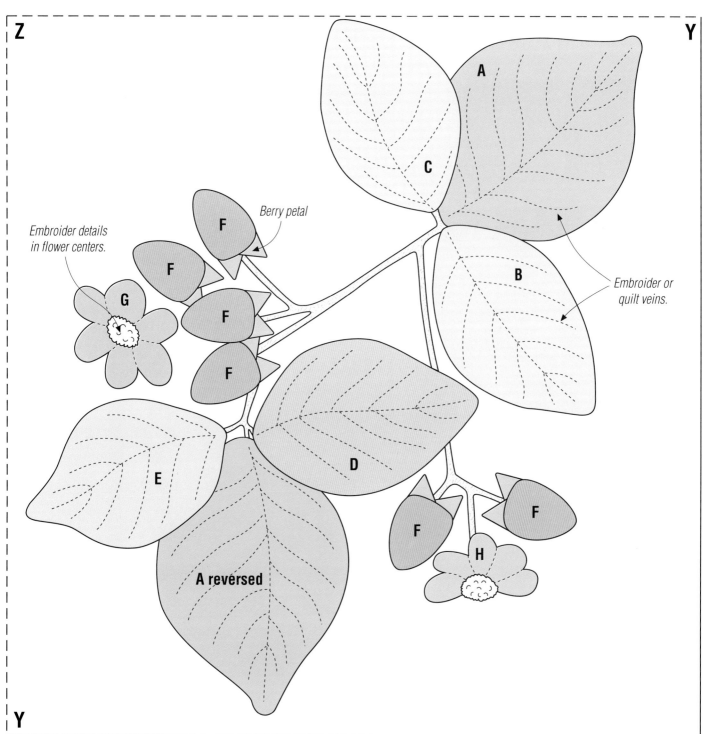

Z

Y

A

C

Berry petal

F

F

Embroider details in flower centers.

G

F

F

B

Embroider or quilt veins.

D

E

A reversed

F

H

F

Y

BLACKBERRY QUADRANT PLAN & TEMPLATES

30" MEDALLION BLOCK

This large medallion block includes leaves, flowers, seeds, and berries from eleven of the wreaths. The block is stunning as a wall hanging, with a simple border or with the special appliqué border that I created especially for it. For a truly spectacular quilt, border the 30" medallion with twelve wreath blocks. Add an appliquéd border and create a prize-winning showstopper!

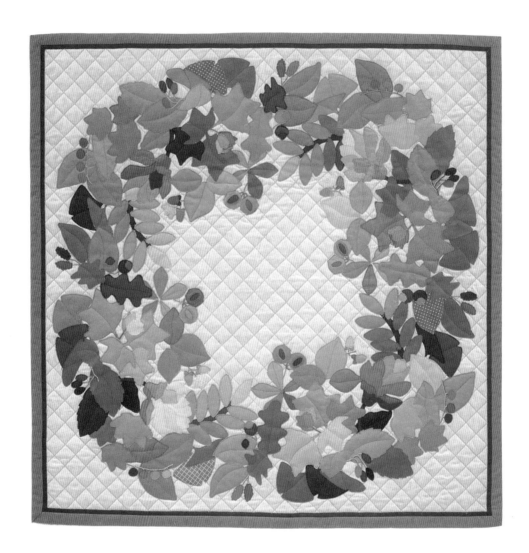

BEFORE YOU CUT

Directions are given for one quadrant of the medallion block. Repeat the appliqué in numerical sequence for each quadrant, noting that the Garry oak and horsechestnut leaves overlap.

See the pullout pattern insert for the quadrant plan. Each piece is identified by the block name and template letter. The numbers in the circles identify the order in which the pieces are to be appliquéd. Appliqué one quadrant at a time or appliqué all steps 1, then steps 2, and so on. Refer to each 15" wreath block for templates and specific appliqué and embroidery instructions.

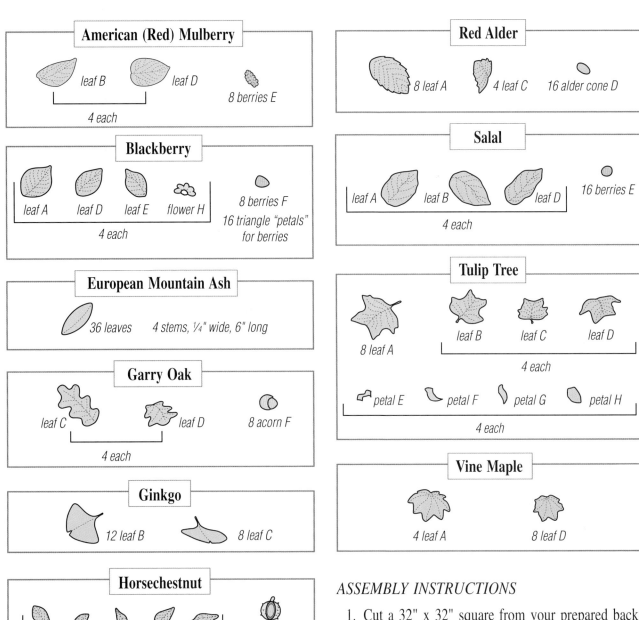

American (Red) Mulberry
leaf B *leaf D* *4 each* *8 berries E*

Blackberry
leaf A *leaf D* *leaf E* *flower H* *4 each* *8 berries F* *16 triangle "petals" for berries*

European Mountain Ash
36 leaves *4 stems, ¼" wide, 6" long*

Garry Oak
leaf C *leaf D* *4 each* *8 acorn F*

Ginkgo
12 leaf B *8 leaf C*

Horsechestnut
leaf J *leaf K* *leaf L* *leaf M* *leaf N* *4 each* *8 seedpods H (double-layer pods)*

Red Alder
8 leaf A *4 leaf C* *16 alder cone D*

Salal
leaf A *leaf B* *leaf D* *4 each* *16 berries E*

Tulip Tree
8 leaf A *leaf B* *leaf C* *leaf D* *4 each* *petal E* *petal F* *petal G* *petal H* *4 each*

Vine Maple
4 leaf A *8 leaf D*

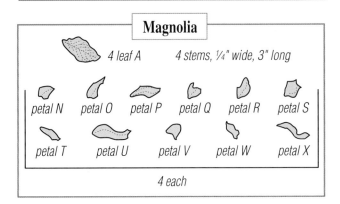

Magnolia
4 leaf A *4 stems, ¼" wide, 3" long*
petal N *petal O* *petal P* *petal Q* *petal R* *petal S*
petal T *petal U* *petal V* *petal W* *petal X*
4 each

ASSEMBLY INSTRUCTIONS

1. Cut a 32" x 32" square from your prepared background fabric. It will be trimmed to 30½" x 30½" when you are finished appliquéing. Prepare the block for appliqué as described on pages 15–17.
2. Appliqué stems, leaves, and magnolia petals in numerical order.
3. Appliqué flowers, berries, buckeyes, cones, and acorns.
4. Refer to the wreath block instructions to embroider flower center, stem, buckeye, berry, and acorn details. Embroider the leaf veins or quilt them later.
5. Trim away the excess background fabric to reduce the bulk.

ASSEMBLING YOUR QUILT TOP

Setting the Blocks

Once your blocks are appliquéd, it's time to set them into a quilt! Arrange them in a way that shows off the colors and values to their best advantage.

Whether the blocks are set side by side, on point, or in a pattern that alternates appliquéd blocks with plain squares, set them to achieve a balance. Each of the blocks has special considerations. Some are light and airy, such as the Pussy Willow or Mountain Ash blocks. Others, such as the Oak or Dogwood blocks, are weighty and nearly cover the entire block with appliqué.

Pin or tape all of your blocks to your design wall and step back to get an overall view. Use a reducing tool (page 13) to spot concentrated areas of color or value. Arrange your blocks in several different combinations to find the grouping you like best.

ADDING THE SASHING

This quilt was designed so that the wreath blocks look stunning without sashing. If you choose to sash your quilt, consider using the same fabric as the background. This increases the space between the blocks and enlarges the quilt. Create a lattice by sashing with narrow strips.

For plain sashing, cut vertical sashing strips the desired width and the same length as the blocks (including seam allowances). Stitch the vertical strips in place between the blocks. Cut horizontal sashing strips the length of the row of sashed blocks and sew the rows together, including a strip at the top and bottom of the quilt. Cut side sashing strips to match the length of the quilt and stitch them to the sides.

An alternative is to sash blocks with sashing squares, which are squares of contrasting fabrics set at the intersection of vertical and horizontal sashing strips. Cut vertical sashing strips the same length as the blocks (including seam allowances). Cut the horizontal sashing strips the same length as the vertical strips. Cut the sashing squares the same dimensions as the width of the sashing strips.

Sew vertical sashing strips to the blocks to make rows, adding a vertical sashing strip on each end of the rows. Alternate the sashing squares with the sashing strips, beginning and ending with the squares. Join the strips to the rows of blocks and include horizontal strips (and squares) at the top and bottom of the blocks.

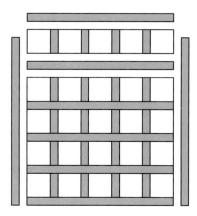

Plain Sashing with Sashing Strips

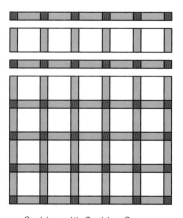

Sashing with Sashing Squares

STRAIGHT SET

Straight-set quilts are the easiest to construct. The term "straight set" refers to blocks that are sewn in rows parallel to the edges of the quilt. After the blocks are sewn in rows, the rows are joined together to assemble the quilt.

1. Square up and trim the blocks so that they all measure 15$\frac{1}{2}$" x 15$\frac{1}{2}$".

2. Sew the blocks together in horizontal rows, using a $\frac{1}{4}$"-wide seam allowance. Measure each block after stitching to check accuracy.

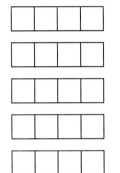

3. With right sides together, pin rows together, matching seams. Stitch. Repeat until you have all the rows sewn together.

TIP

A walking foot or even-feed device (page 29) is helpful when joining blocks and rows, especially those with bias edges. The two layers of fabric are fed through the needle evenly without shifting or puckering.

DIAGONAL SET (ON POINT)

If the blocks are set on point, you will need corner and side triangles to make the quilt rectangular. It helps to lay out all of the blocks and triangles before you start stitching the blocks and rows together.

Note: The following calculations are based on a 15" finished, unsashed block. If you change the size of your block or add sashing, you will need to recalculate the sizes.

Corner Triangles

Corner triangles must be positioned with the square corner (90° angle) cut on grain. This is easy to do by cutting four half-square triangles from two squares. To calculate the size of the square needed to make half-square triangles, divide the finished size of the block (15") by 1.414. This equals 10.61", or 10$\frac{5}{8}$". Next, add 2$\frac{1}{2}$" to equal 13.11" or 13$\frac{1}{8}$". Cut a 13$\frac{1}{8}$" x 13$\frac{1}{8}$" square, then cut it in half diagonally. Sew the bias edge to the end of the block that lies next to the corner. You will have a little extra for trimming later when you square up the finished quilt top.

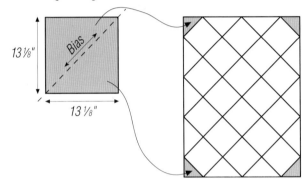

Side Setting Triangles

Side setting triangles are made from large squares that are cut twice diagonally to yield four quarter-square triangles. The long sides of the triangles are on the straight of grain. To calculate the size of the square needed to make quarter-square triangles, multiply the finished size of the block (15") by 1.414. This equals 21.210", or 21$\frac{1}{4}$". Next, add 3" to equal 24.21 or 24$\frac{1}{4}$". Cut a 24$\frac{1}{4}$" x 24$\frac{1}{4}$" square, then cut it twice diagonally. The straight-of-grain sides of the triangles will run along the sides of the quilt. Take care not to stretch the two bias edges when sewing the triangles to the blocks.

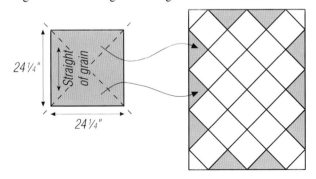

Assembling a Diagonally Set Quilt

1. Square up the blocks so that they all measure 15½" x 15½".
2. Sew the blocks together in diagonal rows, using a ¼"-wide seam allowance. Measure each block after stitching to check accuracy. Press seam allowances in opposite directions from row to row. Add the triangles at the ends of each row.
3. With right sides together, pin rows together, matching seams. Stitch. Take care not to stretch the bias edges of the triangles at the ends of the rows. Add the last two corner triangles. Your quilt will have uneven edges that need to be trimmed. Trim the edges, leaving a ¼"-wide seam allowance.

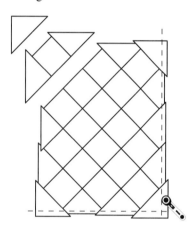

Note: For complete instructions and calculations for sashed and unsashed blocks set on point, refer to *Rotary Riot*, by Judy Hopkins and Nancy J. Martin.

Choosing the Borders

Several appliqué border suggestions and patterns are given in this book. While they greatly enhance the center of the quilt, simple or pieced borders are also beautiful.

When you choose the size of your borders, consider the proportion of the border to the rest of the quilt. Borders that are too narrow may be overpowered by a strong quilt center and won't provide a significant frame for the

quilt. Borders that are too wide dominate the quilt, thereby reducing the impact of the center work and distracting the viewer's eye from what should be the focal point. Similarly, the textures and colors of border fabrics should enhance and support the quilt's center.

Pieced borders read as texture from a distance. If there is high value contrast in the piecework, consider how it blends and coordinates with the center. The size of the pieces must relate to the appliqué motifs within each wreath.

BORDER "TRYOUTS"

Pin the quilt top to your design wall. Fold strips of fabrics that you are considering and pin them under one corner of the quilt. Stand back from the quilt and use your reducing tool to get a full view of how the quilt will look. Try different combinations of fabrics and widths. Even try those fabrics that you wouldn't normally try. Pleasant surprises sometimes occur that "make the quilt." Since your quilt has four corners, you can audition four different combinations at once.

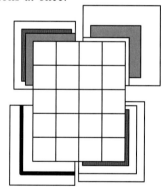

ADDING BORDERS

If you make appliquéd borders, appliqué most of each border before joining it to the quilt. This makes appliqué easier because you do not have to wrestle with the entire quilt. Appliqué to within 6" to 8" of each end of the border strips, stitch the borders to the quilt, then finish the appliqué. The borders may have straight-cut corners or mitered corners. For best results, measure the quilt first, before cutting the border strips.

Straight-Cut Borders

1. Measure the length of the quilt top through the center. Cut side border strips to that measurement, piecing as necessary; mark the centers of the quilt top and the border strips. Pin the borders to the sides of the quilt top, matching the centers and ends and easing as necessary. Sew the border strips in place. Press the seams toward the border.

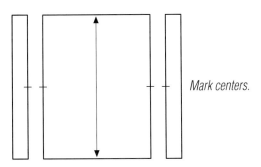

Measure center of quilt, top to bottom.

2. Measure the width of the quilt through the center, including the side borders just added. Cut top and bottom border strips to that measurement, piecing as necessary; mark the center of the quilt top and the border strips. Pin the borders to the sides of the quilt top, matching the centers and ends and easing as necessary. Sew the border strips in place. Press the seams toward the border.

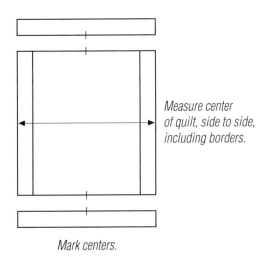

Measure center of quilt, side to side, including borders.

Mark centers.

3. For each succeeding border, measure, cut, pin, and stitch, first the sides, then the top and bottom, until the desired number of borders has been added.

TIP

For a more three-dimensional look, experiment with the direction you press the seam allowances. Combined with quilting in-the-ditch, you can achieve the illusion of depth within the borders' framework.

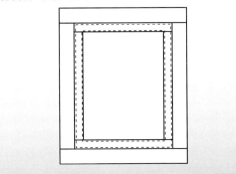

Mitered Corners

1. Estimate the finished outside dimensions of your quilt, including borders. Cut the border strips to this length plus 3" at each end. For example, if your quilt top measures $35\frac{1}{2}$" x $50\frac{1}{2}$" across the center and you want a 6"-wide finished border, your quilt top will measure $47\frac{1}{2}$" x $62\frac{1}{2}$" after the borders are attached to the quilt top.

Note: If your quilt will have multiple borders, sew the individual strips together and treat the resulting unit as a single border strip. This makes mitering corners easier and more accurate. Remember to add the total width of all your borders.

2. Fold the quilt in half and mark the centers of the quilt edges. Fold each border strip in half and mark the centers with pins.

3. Measure the length and width of the quilt across the center. Note the measurements.

4. Place a pin at each end of the side border strips to mark the length of the quilt top. Repeat with the top and bottom borders.

5. Pin the borders to the quilt top, matching the centers. Line up the pins at each end of the border strip with the edges of the quilt. Stitch, beginning and

ending the stitching ¼" from the raw edges of the quilt top. Repeat with the remaining borders.

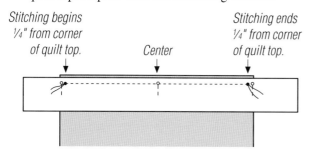

Stitching begins ¼" from corner of quilt top.

Center

Stitching ends ¼" from corner of quilt top.

6. Lay the first corner to be mitered on the ironing board. Fold under one border strip at a 45° angle and adjust as necessary. Press and pin securely.

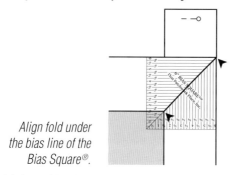

Align fold under the bias line of the Bias Square®.

7. Fold the quilt with right sides together, lining up the edges of the border. If necessary, use a ruler to draw a pencil line on the crease to make the line more visible. Stitch on the pressed crease, sewing from the outside corner to the inside corner. Stop stitching ½ stitch length from the inside corner.

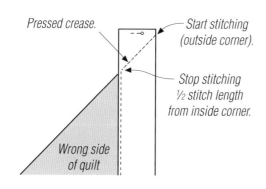

Pressed crease.

Start stitching (outside corner).

Stop stitching ½ stitch length from inside corner.

Wrong side of quilt

8. Press the seam open and trim away excess border fabric, leaving a ¼"-wide seam allowance.

9. Repeat with the remaining corners.

Using the Appliqué Border Plans

The appliqué borders included in the pullout pattern insert are stunning additions to the appliquéd wreath centers of each quilt. Plans for two border widths, one 6"–8" and the other 12", provide options for bordering your quilt with appliqué.

The 6"–8" border is a simpler border, slightly undulating, and can be appliquéd on a wider border strip if you wish. (You will need to adjust yardage requirements if you increase or decrease the width of the borders.)

The 12" border is the more intricate border, featuring leaves, flowers, berries, and seeds from eleven different wreaths (in the three-block border), and twelve different wreaths (in the four- and five-block border).

Each set of plans covers just over half the length of one border. The center section is slightly asymmetrical. The outside leaves of this section signal the transition from the border's asymmetrical section to its symmetrical portion. Remember to flip the pattern over for appliqué placement on the other half.

In addition to a choice of widths, the borders are designed in lengths to match three-, four-, and five-block lengths. All the designs assume that a narrow inner border or combination of borders totaling a 1½" width (finished) surrounds the blocks. Check the plans carefully to determine the proper length for your borders.

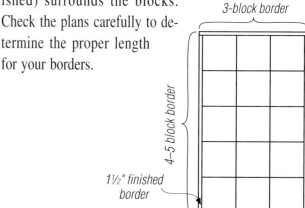

3-block border

4–5 block border

1½" finished border

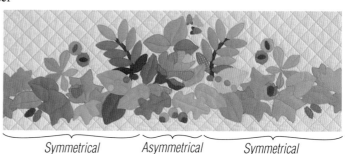

Symmetrical   Asymmetrical   Symmetrical

The 6"–8" border has one design to fit a row of three or four blocks and one design for a five-block row. The 12" border has one design to fit the three-block length and one for the four- and five-block lengths. Of course, you may adapt the three-block border to run along a four- or five-block section.

The 30" medallion-border measurements are based on the inclusion of a 1"-wide (finished) inner border surrounding the central block. The center section of the medallion border is identical to the center section of the 12"-wide border.

Use these borders for design ideas. If your quilt differs in size from the dimensions given here, you will need to shift the leaf template pieces somewhat. Add sections of leaves for longer borders or substitute leaves from other wreaths if you have favorites. If the border plans are too long for your quilt, eliminate a few of the leaves. By changing the configuration of the motifs, you'll make the borders suit the center and unify your work of art.

Appliqué the borders, working from the center to the ends. Appliqué to within 6"–8" of each end of the border strips. After stitching the borders to the quilt, finish the appliqué. Sometimes the appliqué shifts, so minor changes can be made at the corners. The 30" medallion-wreath borders overlap in a corner block, making it necessary to complete appliqué after the borders are attached.

Though the appliqué borders appear to be time-consuming and intricate, my students are surprised at how rapidly the work progresses. The extra effort pays off handsomely when the quilt is finished; the effect is rich, exciting, and truly awesome!

6"- TO 8"-WIDE BORDERS

See the pullout pattern insert for the border plans. Each piece is identified by the wreath block name and the template letter. The numbers in the circles indicate the order in which the pieces are to be appliquéd. Refer to each 15" wreath block for templates and specific appliqué and embroidery instructions.

These border measurements include enough length for a mitered border and assume you will include a $1\frac{1}{2}$"-wide (finished) inner border (or combination of borders totaling $1\frac{1}{2}$") between the blocks and appliquéd border.

For the three-block border, cut each border strip 7" x 66".
For the four-block border, cut each border strip 7" x 81".
For the five-block border, cut each border strip 7" x 96".

Note: If you don't add inner borders or if you use borders of a different width, you will have to alter the appliqué placement by adding or subtracting leaves to fit.

12"-WIDE BORDERS

See the pullout pattern insert for the border plans. Each piece is identified by the wreath block name and the template letter. The numbers in the circles indicate the order in which the pieces are to be appliquéd. Refer to each 15" wreath block for templates and specific appliqué and embroidery instructions.

These border measurements include enough length for a mitered border and assume you will include a $1\frac{1}{2}$"-wide (finished) inner border (or combination of borders totaling $1\frac{1}{2}$") between the blocks and appliquéd border.

For three-block border, cut each border strip 13" x 78".
For four-block border, cut each border strip 13" x 93".
For five-block border, cut each border strip 13" x 108".

Note: If you don't add inner borders or if you use borders of a different width, you will have to alter the appliqué placement by adding or subtracting leaves to fit.

Appliqué Border Motifs

		6"- to 8"-Wide Borders			12"-Wide Borders		30"-Medallion Border	
		3-Block	4-Block	5-Block	3-Block	4- or 5-Block	Each Side Section	Each Corner Section
GINKGO	leaf B	4 / 4r	4 / 4r	4 / 4r	2 / 2r	4 / 4r	—	2 / 2r
	leaf C	2 / 2r	2 / 2r	2 / 2r	1 / 1r	1 / 1r	—	1 / 1r
RED ALDER	leaf A	4 / 4r	4 / 4r	4 / 4r	1 / 1r	2 / 2r	—	2 / 2r
	leaf C	2 / 2r	2 / 2r	2 / 2r	1 / 1r	1 / 1r	—	1 / 1r
	cone D	16	16	16	8	8	—	4
SALAL	leaf A	—	—	—	2 / 2r	1 / 1r	1 / 1r	
	leaf B	1 / 1r	1 / 1r	2 / 2r	3 / 3r	4 / 4r	1 / 1r	
	leaf D	1 / 1r	1 / 1r	2 / 2r	2 / 2r	3 / 3r	1 / 1r	
	berry E	8	8	16	24	24	8	
VINE MAPLE	leaf A	2 / 2r	2 / 2r	2 / 2r	1 / 1r	1 / 1r	1 / 1r	
	leaf D	4 / 4r	4 / 4r	4 / 4r	2 / 2r	2 / 2r	2 / 2r	
FLOWERING DOGWOOD	leaf B		2	2 / 2r	—	2 / 2r	—	
	flower D		1	1	—	1 / 1r	—	
	flower E		1	1	—	1 / 1r	—	
BLACKBERRY	leaf A			1 / 1r	1	1	1	
	leaf D			1 / 1r	1	1	1	
	leaf E			1 / 1r	1	1	1	
	flower H			1 / 1r	1	1	1	
	berry F			4	2	2	2	
	triangle "petals" for berries			8	4	4	4	
AMERICAN (RED) MULBERRY	leaf B				1 / 1r	1 / 1r	1 / 1r	
	leaf D				1 / 1r	1 / 1r	1 / 1r	
	berry E				2 / 2r	2 / 2r	2 / 2r	
EUROPEAN MOUNTAIN ASH	leaves				18	28	18	
	stems, 1/4" wide, 4" long				—	2	—	
	stems, 1/4" wide, 5 1/2" long				2	2	—	
	stems, 1/4" wide, 6" long				—	—	2	
GARRY OAK	leaf C				2 / 2r	2 / 2r	1 / 1r	
	leaf D				1 / 1r	1 / 1r	—	
	acorn F (2 pieces ea.)				7	7	3	
HORSE-CHESTNUT	leaves J, K, L, M, N				1 / 1r	1 / 1r	1 / 1r	
	seedpod H (double-layer pods)				4	4	4	
MAGNOLIA	leaf A				3	3	3	
	flower petals N, O, P, Q, R, S, T, U, V, W, X				1	1	1	
	stems, 1/4" wide, 1" long				1	1	1	
TULIP TREE	leaf A				2 / 2r	2 / 2r	2 / 2r	
	leaf B				1 / 1r	1 / 1r	1 / 1r	
	leaf D				1 / 1r	1 / 1r	1 / 1r	
	flower petals E, F, G, H				1 / 1r	1 / 1r	1 / 1r	

Appliqué Border Motifs

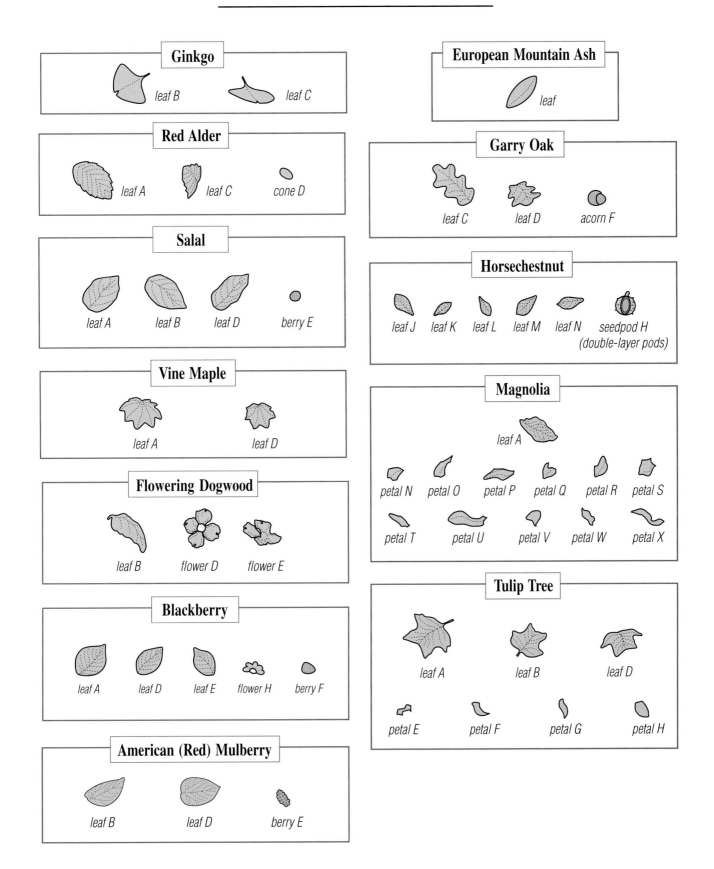

Ginkgo

leaf B   leaf C

European Mountain Ash

leaf

Red Alder

leaf A   leaf C   cone D

Garry Oak

leaf C   leaf D   acorn F

Salal

leaf A   leaf B   leaf D   berry E

Horsechestnut

leaf J   leaf K   leaf L   leaf M   leaf N   seedpod H
(double-layer pods)

Vine Maple

leaf A   leaf D

Magnolia

leaf A

petal N   petal O   petal P   petal Q   petal R   petal S

petal T   petal U   petal V   petal W   petal X

Flowering Dogwood

leaf B   flower D   flower E

Blackberry

leaf A   leaf D   leaf E   flower H   berry F

Tulip Tree

leaf A   leaf B   leaf D

petal E   petal F   petal G   petal H

American (Red) Mulberry

leaf B   leaf D   berry E

THREE-BLOCK, 6"- TO 8"-WIDE BORDER

The three-block, 6"- to 8"-wide border does not include the Flowering Dogwood motif, as does the four-block, 6"-wide border. Joan Dawson was able to fit the four-block border on a three-block-wide quilt by making the border 8" wide. (See quilt on page 42.)

Appliqué and Assembly

Directions are for half of the border. For the other half, appliqué in the same order but *be sure to reverse the templates.* Each piece is identified by the block name and template letter. The numbers in the circles identify the order in which the pieces are to be appliquéd. Refer to each 15" wreath block for templates and specific appliqué and embroidery instructions.

1. Appliqué the leaves as indicated on the border plan. Do not appliqué the outer red alder leaves and the outer ginkgo leaves yet.
2. Appliqué the second half of the border.
3. Stitch the borders to the quilt, mitering the corners. (See pages 101–102.)
4. Lay the remaining appliqué pieces on the borders to make sure they align properly in the corners. If necessary, adjust the space between the outermost leaves to get a pleasing effect. You may add leaves of your choice to lengthen the appliqué section.
5. Appliqué the outer red alder and ginkgo leaves in the order indicated on the border plan.
6. Appliqué the salal berries and red alder cones.
7. Embroider the stem, berry, and cone details as desired. Embroider the leaf veins or quilt them later. (See pages 32–34 for embroidery stitches.)
8. Carefully trim away the excess background fabric to reduce the bulk.

FOUR-BLOCK, 6"- TO 8"-WIDE BORDER

Appliqué and Assembly

Directions are for half of the border. For the other half, appliqué in the same order but *be sure to reverse the templates.*

1. Appliqué dogwood leaves and flowers in the order indicated on the border plan.
2. Complete the border, following steps 1–8 of the three-block, 6"-wide border on page 106.

FIVE-BLOCK, 6"- TO 8"-WIDE BORDER

Appliqué and Assembly

Directions are given to complete the center motif of dogwood flowers and leaves and for half of the border. For the other half, appliqué in the same order but *be sure to reverse the templates.* Each piece is identified by the block name and template letter. The numbers in the circles identify the order in which the pieces are to be appliquéd. Refer to each 15" wreath block for templates and specific appliqué and embroidery instructions.

1. Appliqué the leaves and flowers as indicated on the border plan. Do not appliqué the outer red alder leaves and ginkgo leaves yet.
2. Appliqué the blackberries, blackberry flower, and salal berries next.

3. Appliqué the second half of the border.
4. After all four borders are appliquéd, stitch them to the quilt, mitering the corners. (See pages 101–102.)
5. Appliqué the outer red alder and ginkgo leaves in the order indicated on the border plan.
6. Appliqué the red alder cones.
7. Embroider the stem, flower, berry, and cone details as desired. Embroider the leaf veins or quilt them later if you wish.
8. Carefully trim away the excess background fabric to reduce the bulk.

Appliqué and Assembly

Directions are given for half of the border. For the other half, appliqué in the same order but *be sure to reverse the templates.* Each piece is identified by the block name and template letter. The numbers in the circles identify the appliqué order. Refer to each 15" wreath block for templates and specific appliqué and embroidery instructions.

1. Appliqué the leaves, stems, and flowers as indicated on the border plan. Do not appliqué the outer red alder leaves and ginkgo leaves.
2. Appliqué the mulberries, blackberries and flower, acorns, buckeyes, salal berries, and tulip tree flower. Do not appliqué the red alder cones yet.
3. Appliqué the second half of the border.
4. After all four borders are appliquéd, stitch them to the quilt, mitering the corners. (See pages 101–102.)
5. Lay the remaining appliqué pieces on the borders to make sure they align properly in the corners. If necessary, adjust the space between the outermost leaves to get a pleasing effect. You may add leaves of your choice to lengthen the appliqué section.
6. Appliqué the outer red alder and ginkgo leaves in the order indicated on the border plan.
7. Appliqué the red alder cones.
8. Embroider the stem, flower, buckeye, berry, and acorn details as desired. Embroider leaf veins or quilt them later.
9. Carefully trim away the excess background fabric to reduce the bulk.

FOUR- OR FIVE-BLOCK, 12"-WIDE BORDER

Appliqué and Assembly

Directions are given for half of the border. For the other half, appliqué in the same order but *be sure to reverse the templates*. Each piece is identified by the block name and template letter. The numbers in the circles identify the order in which the pieces are to be appliquéd. Refer to each 15" wreath block for templates and specific appliqué and embroidery instructions.

1. Appliqué the leaves, stems, and flowers as indicated on the border plan. Do not appliqué the outer red alder leaves and ginkgo leaves yet.
2. Appliqué the mulberries, blackberries and flower, acorns, buckeyes, salal berries, and tulip tree flower. Do not appliqué the red alder cones yet.
3. Appliqué the second half of the border.

4. After all four borders are appliquéd, stitch them to the quilt, mitering the corners. (See pages 101–102.)
5. Lay the remaining appliqué pieces on the borders to make sure they align properly in the corners. If necessary, adjust the space between the outermost leaves to get a pleasing effect. You may add leaves of your choice to lengthen the appliqué section.
6. Appliqué the outer red alder and ginkgo leaves in the order indicated on the border plan.
7. Appliqué the red alder cones.
8. Embroider the stem, flower, buckeye, berry, and acorn details as desired. Embroider leaf veins or quilt them later.
9. Carefully trim away the excess background fabric to reduce the bulk.

BORDER FOR 30" MEDALLION BLOCK

Side Border Section

Corner Section

Assembling Your Quilt Top

MEDALLION BORDERS

The 12"-wide border for the 30" medallion block is similar to the 12"-wide borders for three-, four-, and five-block borders. Since it is designed for a 30" block with a 1"-wide inner border, it can also be used as a two-block border as well, framing four 15" wreaths (including a 1"-wide inner border).

This border was designed to be appliquéd in two units: sides and corners. See the pullout pattern insert for the border plans. Each piece is identified by the block name and the template letter. The numbers in the circles indicate the order in which the pieces are to be appliquéd. The side border sections should be appliquéd first, between and including the sets of vine maple leaves. Appliqué the corner sections and the remaining pieces of the side sections *after* the borders have been stitched to the quilt. Refer to each 15" wreath block for templates and specific appliqué and embroidery instructions.

Cut each border strip 13" x 62". This includes enough length for a mitered border and assumes you will include a 1"-wide inner border (or combination of borders totaling 1") between the blocks and the appliquéd border. If you don't add inner borders or if you add borders of a different width, you will have to alter the appliqué by adding or subtracting leaves.

Appliqué and Assembly

Directions are for half of the border. For the other half, appliqué in the same order but *be sure to reverse the templates*. Each piece is identified by the block name and template letter. The numbers in the circles identify the order in which the pieces are to be appliquéd. Refer to each 15" wreath block for templates and specific appliqué and embroidery instructions.

1. Appliqué the leaves, stems, and flower as indicated on the border plan. Do not appliqué the outer red alder leaves and ginkgo leaves yet.
2. Appliqué the mulberries, blackberries and flower, acorns, buckeyes, salal berries, and tulip tree flower. Do not appliqué the red alder cones yet.
3. After all four border sections are appliquéd, stitch the borders to the quilt, mitering the corners. (See pages 101–102.)
4. Before appliquéing the corner sections, lay the corner appliqué pieces on the borders to make sure they are spaced properly. If necessary, adjust the space between the pieces.
5. Appliqué the red alder and ginkgo leaves in each corner in the order indicated on the border plan.
6. Appliqué the red alder cones.
7. Embroider the stems, flower, buckeye, berry, and acorn details as desired. Embroider the leaf veins or quilt them later.
8. Carefully trim away the excess background fabric to reduce the bulk.

Finishing Your Quilt

Backing

Fabric for quilt backs should be compatible with the quilt top. I prefer 100% cotton. It is possible to find fabric in widths of 90" or more, which are wide enough to use without having to piece the back.

Make pieced backs from leftover blocks, photos (fabric transfers), or other fabrics that have special meaning to the quilt or to the intended recipient. Many exciting ideas are included on the backs of quilts, so it is tempting to peek behind each one at exhibits just to make sure you're not missing anything!

Always make the backing larger than the quilt top to allow for shifting of the layers during quilting. Make backings 2" larger than the quilt top on all sides.

Press the backing before you layer it with the batting and quilt top.

Batting

Batting comes in many sizes, weights, and fiber contents. Polyester battings are lightweight and easy to quilt through. They don't need to be as closely quilted as natural fiber battings do, and polyester is resistant to insect damage. In addition to white, polyester batting is available in black, which is nice for dark quilts.

Cotton and polyester/cotton combination battings require quilting lines set close together, and they impart a traditional, old-fashioned quality to the quilt.

Wool battings are expensive but lovely to quilt through. They too must be more closely quilted.

Flannel may be used, but the fabric must be laundered and dried in the dryer many times before it stops shrinking. It is also very important to align its grain line exactly with the grain line of the quilt top and backing, or it won't fold without twisting.

Follow the manufacturers' recommendations for pretreating all battings. Also, let batting "relax" on a flat surface for a day or two before you cut it to size. Cut the batting at least 2" larger than the quilt top on all sides.

Quilting

Quilting imparts dimension and texture—qualities that add warmth and life to your quilt. It is every bit as important as the quilt's appliqué or piecework. The quilting pattern should enhance and enliven without competing, achieving a balance that is a joy to behold.

These wreaths come to life when they are quilted. When the leaf veins are quilted, the leaves appear startlingly real. (See Joan Dawson's quilt on page 42.) Outlining the leaves, stems, flowers, and berries makes them appear to float away from the background, ready to be plucked from the quilt!

Complex quilting designs are not necessary in the background areas. A simple grid or series of straight lines is sufficient to support the intricate appliqué.

One option is to quilt plain blocks that alternate with appliquéd blocks, using wreath designs from this book that you did not appliqué. Or, use motifs from the wreaths for quilting designs in the sashing strips or borders.

Don't overlook the possibilities traditional quilting patterns offer. For an elaborate look, try working feathered quilting patterns into plain blocks and/or borders.

MARKING QUILTING PATTERNS

Mark the quilting lines on the entire quilt top before basting and quilting, or mark only the area that you will quilt in one sitting, whichever you prefer. (See page 13 for information on marking tools.)

Masking tape is a useful guide for quilting a series of lines or a grid. The $^3/_4$"-wide tape is a perfect grid size. Make sure the masking tape is fresh; it becomes gummy with age, and old tape will leave a messy residue on the quilt. Stick it to some muslin a few times as you pull it from the roll to "fuzz it up" before placing it on the quilt. Masking tape can be reused several times before it becomes too fuzzy to stick. Be very careful when you remove the tape, especially from embroidered areas.

LAYERING THE QUILT

1. Lay the backing wrong side up on a large, flat surface. Smooth out all the wrinkles, working from the center out. Tape it to the work surface to hold it taut but not stretched.
2. Lay the batting on top of the backing and pat out any wrinkles.
3. Lay the pressed quilt top on top of the batting. Make sure the backing and batting extend equally around all four sides. Smooth out any wrinkles, again working from the center out.
4. Pin the layers together every 6" with long quilting or safety pins. Work from the center out.
5. Baste the layers together vertically and horizontally. Space the rows 4" apart and use long stitches ($^1/_4$"–$^1/_2$" long). Remove the pins as you go.

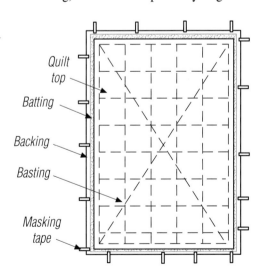

Quilt top

Batting

Backing

Basting

Masking tape

TIP

1. Fold the backing over the quilt top to enclose the batting. This keeps the batting from catching and tearing.
2. Then baste 6"- to 8"-wide strips of muslin along the quilt-top edges after layering. This extends the amount of fabric that is held in the quilt hoop or frame so that quilting can be easily carried out to the edges of the quilt. After I am done quilting, I remove the basting and reuse the muslin strips on the next quilt.

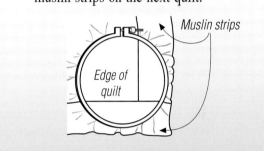

Muslin strips

Edge of quilt

HAND QUILTING

I prefer using cotton and cotton/polyester threads that are made specifically for hand quilting. They are durable, resist knotting, and are easy to thread through a needle.

The shorter the quilting needle you work with, the shorter your stitches will be. Generally quilting is done with needles called Betweens, sizes 10, 11, or 12. I prefer size 11 Betweens with large eyes, which are easier to thread.

I use two thimbles when I quilt. I wear a thimble with a raised brass ring around the tip, on the middle finger of my quilting hand. Under the quilt, I wear a regular thimble on my middle finger. I use the edge of the thimble tip to push up against the quilt, which forms a ridge to guide the needle. I find I can take much smaller stitches using this ridge-making technique.

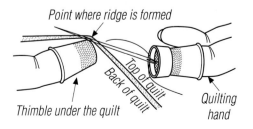

Point where ridge is formed

Top of quilt

Back of quilt

Thimble under the quilt

Quilting hand

There are many different quilting hoops and frames available to hold the quilt layers taut while stitching. I prefer round hoops with tightening screws because they maintain an even tension. Experiment to find the type you prefer.

The Hand Quilting Stitch

The quilting stitch is actually a running stitch, made with small stitches of even lengths. Always start quilting in the center of the quilt and work out to the sides.

1. Knot an 18" length of quilting thread with a very small knot. Insert the needle through the quilt top and batting about 1" from where you want to begin quilting. Bury the knot in the batting by pulling gently until it pops through the top layer.
2. Take a tiny backstitch, then continue stitching along the quilting line. Check occasionally to make sure the stitch goes all the way through to the back.
3. Quilt to within the last stitch and make a tiny knot in the thread. Bury the knot and bring the needle out to the top, taking about a $^1/_2$"–$^3/_4$" stitch inside the batting. Clip the thread.

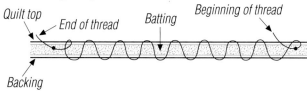

Quilt top · End of thread · Batting · Beginning of thread · Backing

MACHINE QUILTING

Machine quilting gives a quilt a more defined line element than hand quilting. For quilts that will be heavily used, machine quilting is generally more durable. The most important tool for machine quilting (other than a sewing machine in good working order) is a walking foot or even-feed feature (page 29). As with machine appliqué, a walking foot helps feed the quilt layers through the machine without shifting or puckering.

Monofilament nylon is often used for machine quilting. It comes in two colors that blend well with all fabrics. It is strong and appropriate for heavy-use quilts. However, I prefer 100% cotton or cotton-wrapped polyester thread.

As with hand-quilted quilts, begin machine quilting in the center of the quilt and work to the outer edges.

1. Begin stitching, using a 0 stitch length, and make three or four stitches in one place. (This makes a series of knots.) Then, increase the stitch length to 10–12 stitches per inch and sew along the quilting line until you reach the end. Decrease the stitch length to 0, making the last three or four stitches in one place. Be sure the layers do not pucker or develop tucks as they go through the machine. Stop frequently to check and adjust if necessary.

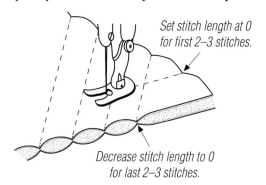

Set stitch length at 0 for first 2–3 stitches.

Decrease stitch length to 0 for last 2–3 stitches.

Note: Some quiltmakers drop the feed dog and make three or four stitches at the beginning, then raise the feed dog and stitch to the end. They then drop the feed dog again and stitch in place.

2. Clip the thread ends on the front and back of the quilt, being careful not to cut the knots.

For a knot-free appearance on the surface of the quilt, try the following method. It is time-consuming but yields beautiful results.

1. Begin and end all lines of machine quilting with a stitch length of 10–12 stitches per inch. Leave a 2" thread "tail."
2. Turn the quilt over and pull all the thread tails from the front of the quilt through to the back.

Quilt back
Quilt front

3. Tie off each pair of threads with a square knot (right thread over left thread, then left thread over right thread). Be sure the knot is tied right next to the quilt's surface.

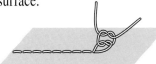

4. Thread both knot ends through a large-eyed needle and insert the needle tip into the quilt as close to the knot as possible. (Sometimes, if the thread ends are too short, I bury the tip of the needle into the quilt first, then thread it and pull it through.)

5. Run the needle inside the quilt for about 2" in an area free of quilting, burying the knot ends inside the quilt.
6. Bring the needle out the quilt back and clip off any remaining thread ends at the surface of the quilt.

Back
Batting
Front

Binding

Adding the binding to a quilt is an exciting moment for me. I experience a sense of accomplishment when I make the final stitches.

Binding can either be cut on the straight grain or on the bias. I prefer to bind all my quilts with double-fold binding made from $1^7/_8$"-wide bias strips. (See page 18 for instructions on cutting bias strips.) Use your favorite binding method. Refer to *Happy Endings* by Mimi Dietrich for step-by-step binding directions.

Labels

Always label your quilts with your name, the year the quilt was completed, and town and state where it was completed!

Consider making your label more elaborate by including a couple of the appliqué design elements from the front of the quilt. If you have a favorite flower or tree motif, add one to your label.

Additional information that you include will be welcome documentation for those who view your work in the years to come. Please take the time to credit yourself for the work you have put into your quilt. Your family, friends, and someday, heirs, will be glad you did.

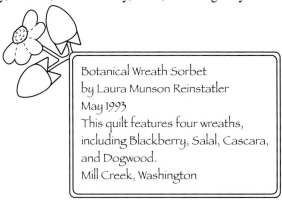

Botanical Wreath Sorbet
by Laura Munson Reinstatler
May 1993
This quilt features four wreaths,
including Blackberry, Salal, Cascara,
and Dogwood.
Mill Creek, Washington

Hanging Your Quilt

Take the time to make a fabric sleeve to hang your quilt. Even if you plan to keep your quilt on a bed, it is a good idea to add a sleeve to the back in case you decide to exhibit the quilt in the future. It takes very little time and effort, and it ensures against uneven stretching.

1. Cut a strip of fabric 10" wide and as long as the top edge of the quilt, less 1".
2. Fold the strip in half lengthwise, right sides together. Stitch $1/_4$" from the raw edges to make a long sleeve. Turn the sleeve right side out. Press.

3. Hem the ends by turning under $1/_4$", then $1/_4$" again. Stitch close to the inner folded edge.

4. Lay the sleeve on the back of the quilt along the top edge. Place the sleeve's seam along the center of the sleeve, against the quilt. Position the top of the sleeve 1/4" below the binding. Beginning 6" from each end of the sleeve, lower the sleeve so that it will be 1/2" away from the binding as shown. I learned this trick from a gallery owner. It helps decrease the wavy look that sometimes happens along the bottom edge of a quilt when it is hanging.

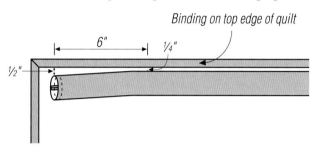

Binding on top edge of quilt

5. Blindstitch the top edge of the sleeve to the quilt, making sure your stitches do not go through to the front of the quilt.

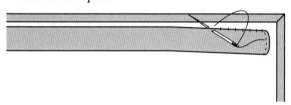

6. Raise the lower edge of the sleeve about 1/2" to create some give for the hanging rod and so the hanging rod does not put strain on the quilt. Blindstitch or tack along the sleeve's lower edge.

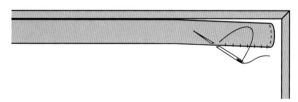

Push sleeve up 1/2" and stitch bottom edge.

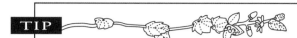

TIP

Stitch 2" sections every 4" or so along the sleeve's lower edge. This prevents a line from showing on the front of the quilt.

Note: If you have a very wide quilt, make two or three shorter sleeve sections instead of one long one. This prevents a heavier quilt hanging on a narrow rod from sagging if you use hooks to support the rod where the sleeve sections come together.

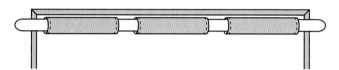

AFTERWORD

After teaching many "Botanical Wreaths" classes and creating several quilts, I have developed new appreciation and deeper reverence for our botanical surroundings. My awareness of the subtleties of nature increased while working on these projects. I now know the greens include a vast range of hues—more subtle than I ever before imagined. With the change in seasons, these greens transform into a multitude of colors representing all points of the spectrum. Flowers, seeds, berries, and stems provide additional richness to the botanical palette.

I love appliqué. Auditioning the colors brings me pleasure as they blend and dance. Moving the window template over the fabric, finding the perfect spot for a leaf or berry, laying each new piece on the block—all contribute to the joy. A special peace envelops me as I take each tiny stitch in the quilt.

Expressing the beauty found in nature through quiltmaking is an enormously rewarding experience. My students report similar feelings while working on their botanical quilts. If a Botanical Wreath project seems daunting at first, remember: Each of the quilts in this book was made just one stitch at a time. As you work on your quilt, take the time to reflect on the beauty around you. Surely, the magic and grace of nature will enter gently into your work.

NOTES

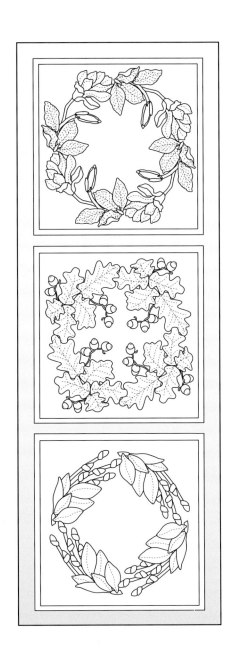

MEET THE AUTHOR

*L*aura Munson Reinstatler began using scissors, pins, needles, and thread at an early age, first sewing doll clothes, then clothes for herself. Later, she combined her love of fiber and drawing, obtaining a degree in art with a textile emphasis at the University of Washington. She then studied for a time with a weaver in Denmark. Laura began quilting full time in 1980, exploring color interactions within the framework of Seminole and strip-piecing techniques.

Her work evolved into the miniature strip-piecing technique for which she is known, although in the past few years, her quilting journey has taken her into the realm of appliqué.

Laura works as an editor for That Patchwork Place, and considers herself fortunate to combine two loves—writing and quilts. She lives in the Seattle area with husband Bob and son Colin. Living in the heart of the Pacific Northwest, she enjoys the botanical wonders of the native flora that grows so prolifically there.

That Patchwork Place Publications and Products

BOOKS

All the Blocks Are Geese by Mary Sue Suit
Angle Antics by Mary Hickey
Animas Quilts by Jackie Robinson
Appliqué Borders: An Added Grace by Jeana Kimball
Appliquilt: Whimsical One-Step Appliqué by Tonee White
Baltimore Bouquets by Mimi Dietrich
Basket Garden by Mary Hickey
Biblical Blocks by Rosemary Makhan
Blockbuster Quilts by Margaret J. Miller
Botanical Wreaths by Laura M. Reinstatler
Calendar Quilts by Joan Hanson
Cathedral Window: A Fresh Look by Nancy J. Martin
The Cat's Meow by Janet Kime
Colourwash Quilts by Deirdre Amsden
Corners in the Cabin by Paulette Peters
Country Medallion Sampler by Carol Doak
Country Threads by Connie Tesene and Mary Tendall
Easy Machine Paper Piecing by Carol Doak
Easy Quilts...By Jupiter® by Mary Beth Maison
Even More by Trudie Hughes
Fantasy Flowers by Doreen Cronkite Burbank
Fit To Be Tied by Judy Hopkins
Five- and Seven-Patch Blocks & Quilts for the ScrapSaver
   by Judy Hopkins
Four-Patch Blocks & Quilts for the ScrapSaver
   by Judy Hopkins
Fun with Fat Quarters by Nancy J. Martin
Go Wild with Quilts by Margaret Rolfe
Handmade Quilts by Mimi Dietrich
Happy Endings by Mimi Dietrich
Holiday Happenings by Christal Carter
Home for Christmas by Nancy J. Martin and Sharon Stanley
In The Beginning by Sharon Evans Yenter
Irma's Sampler by Irma Eskes
Jacket Jazz by Judy Murrah
Lessons in Machine Piecing by Marsha McCloskey
Little By Little: Quilts in Miniature by Mary Hickey
Little Quilts by Alice Berg, Sylvia Johnson, and
   Mary Ellen Von Holt
Lively Little Logs by Donna McConnell
Loving Stitches by Jeana Kimball
Make Room for Quilts by Nancy J. Martin
More Template-Free® Quiltmaking by Trudie Hughes
Nifty Ninepatches by Carolann M. Palmer
Nine-Patch Blocks & Quilts for the ScrapSaver by Judy Hopkins
Not Just Quilts by Jo Parrott

On to Square Two by Marsha McCloskey
Osage County Quilt Factory by Virginia Robertson
Painless Borders by Sally Schneider
A Perfect Match by Donna Lynn Thomas
Picture Perfect Patchwork by Naomi Norman
Piecemakers® Country Store by the Piecemakers
Pineapple Passion by Nancy Smith and Lynda Milligan
A Pioneer Doll and Her Quilts by Mary Hickey
Pioneer Storybook Quilts by Mary Hickey
Prairie People—Cloth Dolls to Make and Cherish by Marji
   Hadley and J. Dianne Ridgley
Quick & Easy Quiltmaking by Mary Hickey, Nancy J. Martin,
   Marsha McCloskey and Sara Nephew
Quilted for Christmas compiled by Ursula Reikes
The Quilters' Companion compiled by That Patchwork Place
The Quilting Bee by Jackie Wolff and Lori Aluna
Quilts for All Seasons by Christal Carter
Quilts for Baby: Easy as A, B, C by Ursula Reikes
Quilts for Kids by Carolann M. Palmer
Quilts from Nature by Joan Colvin
Quilts to Share by Janet Kime
Red and Green: An Appliqué Tradition by Jeana Kimball
Red Wagon Originals by Gerry Kimmel and Linda Brannock
Rotary Riot by Judy Hopkins and Nancy J. Martin
Rotary Roundup by Judy Hopkins and Nancy J. Martin
Round About Quilts by J. Michelle Watts
Samplings from the Sea by Rosemary Makhan
Scrap Happy by Sally Schneider
ScrapMania by Sally Schneider
Sensational Settings by Joan Hanson
Sewing on the Line by Lesly-Claire Greenberg
Shortcuts: A Concise Guide to Rotary Cutting
   by Donna Lynn Thomas (metric version available)
Shortcuts Sampler by Roxanne Carter
Shortcuts to the Top by Donna Lynn Thomas
Small Talk by Donna Lynn Thomas
Smoothstitch™ Quilts by Roxi Eppler
The Stitchin' Post by Jean Wells and Lawry Thorn
Strips That Sizzle by Margaret J. Miller
Sunbonnet Sue All Through the Year by Sue Linker
Tea Party Time by Nancy J. Martin
Template-Free® Quiltmaking by Trudie Hughes
Template-Free® Quilts and Borders by Trudie Hughes
Template-Free® Stars by Jo Parrott
Watercolor Quilts by Pat Magaret and Donna Slusser
Women and Their Quilts by Nancyann Johanson Twelker

TOOLS

6" Bias Square®	BiRangle™	Rotary Rule™
8" Bias Square®	Pineapple Rule	Ruby Beholder™
Metric Bias Square®	Rotary Mate™	ScrapMaster

VIDEO

Shortcuts to America's Best-Loved Quilts

Many titles are available at your local quilt shop. For more information, send $2 for a color catalog to That Patchwork Place, Inc., PO Box 118, Bothell WA 98041-0118 USA.

☎ Call 1-800-426-3126 for the name and location of the quilt shop nearest you.